IMAGES OF WAR SPECIAL

TIGER I AND TIGER II

A German and a Hungarian share a cigarette next to the imposing bulk of the Tiger II.

IMAGES OF WAR SPECIAL

TIGER I AND TIGER II

RARE PHOTOGRAPHS FROM WARTIME ARCHIVES

Anthony Tucker-Jones

Illustrated by
Brian Delf

Pen & Sword
MILITARY

First published in Great Britain in 2012
and reprinted in 2014, 2016 and 2017 by
PEN AND SWORD MILITARY
An imprint of
Pen & Sword Books Ltd
47 Church Street, Barnsley
South Yorkshire
S70 2AS

ISBN 978 1 78159 030 0

Printed and bound in India
by Replika Press Pvt. Ltd.

Pen & Sword Books Ltd incorporates the Imprints of Pen & Sword Aviation,
Pen & Sword Family History, Pen & Sword Maritime, Pen & Sword Military,
Pen & Sword Discovery, Pen & Sword Politics, Pen & Sword Atlas,
Pen & Sword Archaeology, Wharncliffe Local History, Leo Cooper,
Wharncliffe True Crime, Wharncliffe Transport, Pen & Sword Select,
Pen & Sword Military Classics, The Praetorian Press, Claymore Press,
Remember When, Seaforth Publishing and Frontline Publishing

For a complete list of Pen & Sword titles please contact
PEN & SWORD BOOKS LIMITED
47 Church Street, Barnsley, South Yorkshire, S70 2AS, England
E-mail: enquiries@pen-and-sword.co.uk
Website: www.pen-and-sword.co.uk

Contents

Introduction: Hitler's Zoo

This book sets out to chart the remarkable story of the Tiger I and II tanks. Adolf Hitler's Panzerwaffe (panzer force) named most of its tanks and armoured fighting vehicles after wild animals, including big cats. The Tiger tanks were no exception and on paper were war-winning designs. The name also conjures up an image of savagery and brutal killing. Such is its fame that if you ask anyone to name a tank, they will inevitably say the Tiger. But frankly, though it might be heresy, both the Tiger I and II are overrated.

In reality the Tigers were over-engineered, required raw materials that were in very short supply, were time-consuming to produce and difficult to recover from the battlefield. They were very heavy, not altogether reliable and vulnerable on the flanks. Even so, their thick armour gave them survivability and their main gun enabled them to stand off and kill their enemies with ease. It was these two traits that most frightened Allied tankers. Nonetheless, despite its later reputation, the Tiger I's debut in Russia and Tunisia was far from auspicious.

The myth of the 'invincible' Tiger has developed over time and it is often considered the deadliest tank of the Second World War. Certainly at the time British and American tankers developed 'Tiger anxiety'. The reality is somewhat different: with only 1,354 Tiger Is and around 500 Tiger IIs ever built, they were never going to achieve anything more than a local impact on the conduct of the war. In contrast, the Panzer Mk III/IV, M4 Sherman and T-34 tanks were produced in the tens of thousands. Almost 6,000 Panzer Mk V Panthers were manufactured, and this was an immediate contemporary of the Tiger. Variants of the Tiger were built in even more limited numbers: there were only seventy-seven Jagdtigers, eighteen Sturmpanzers and ninety Jagdpanzer Elefants. Recovery vehicles consisted of just three Bergepanzer Tiger Is and three Bergepanzer Elefants.

When Pen & Sword approached me to write a new profile of the legendary Tiger tank, I was somewhat hesitant. After all, what more can be said about what is easily the most famous (or infamous) tank of the Second World War. Its status remains undiminished and certainly, no matter how you look at it, the Tiger was a tank-killer par excellence. It has been calculated that some 1,800 Tigers accounted for almost 9,000 kills.

Every schoolboy growing up with an interest in military history invariably ends up with a model Tiger tank on his shelves. I must confess I still possess to this very day a 1/72-scale Airfix Tiger that I built way back in the 1970s. Those with an interest in such matters know that it took at least three Allied tanks to knock out a single Tiger and that it was the scourge of the Allies in the bloody battles for Normandy. Therein, though, lies the fallacy of the Tiger's fame: no matter how many Shermans or T-34 tanks it knocked out, the American, British and Soviet armies always had more.

Is it possible to offer a fresh perspective on the history of the Tiger tank? For such an iconic tank its position is pretty much unassailable. Phrases such as 'the secret history' or 'the untold story' are hollow marketing enticements that crop up with regular monotony. It is, though, possible, by marshalling the evidence and technical assessments, to help re-evaluate perceptions and indeed misconceptions of the role of the Tiger in the evolution of armoured warfare.

All rather highbrow perhaps, but the key questions are where was it deployed, how was it deployed and what was its impact? Understand these and you can understand the contribution of any tank. This can then be boiled down to an even simpler question: did the tank fulfil the role it was intended for. Ultimately, the answer for the Tiger is a resounding no, though some may beg to differ.

I first became closely acquainted with the Tiger's capabilities through a very long-standing fascination with the Normandy campaign and subsequently through an interest with the campaigns fought in North Africa and on the Eastern Front. On closer inspection, it soon becomes apparent that the Tiger's reputation is built upon its quite remarkable tactical success and no more. There can be no denying that there were simply too few Tiger Is and even fewer Tiger IIs to make a difference to the outcome of the war. In addition, the Tiger was designed as a heavy breakthrough tank and yet it ended up being used in environments that did not play to its strengths and increasingly in a defensive role.

All the Tiger did was help slow down what, after the summer of 1944, was the inevitable defeat of Nazi Germany. If Hitler's factories had had the wherewithal to gear up to produce just Tiger tanks, then the Second World War might have turned out very differently. The reality is that they were never in a position to do so.

The German High Command without a doubt squandered its opportunities with the Tiger. Rather than equip an entire panzer division with it, the Tigers were dissipated into piecemeal penny packets among the German Army and Waffen-SS. Because there were so few of them, they were formed into independent tank battalions that enabled a very powerful tactical blow, but lacked a greater strategic punch.

Hitler – always his own worst enemy – could not wait to get the Tiger into action and pointlessly committed a few first at Leningrad and then in Tunisia, where the local terrain did not allow it to play to its strengths. It also meant that the Allies soon became aware of the presence of a new and formidable German panzer. Similarly at the Battle of Kursk, which is often cited as the Tiger's finest moment, again there were too few. Likewise the impact of the subsequent Tiger II in Normandy, at the Battle of the Bulge and at Budapest/Lake Balaton was very limited.

The paucity and wasteful deployment of the Tiger caused rancour among Hitler's senior generals. General Heinz Guderian, father of Hitler's panzer forces and Inspector General of Armoured Forces, was dismayed at how they were wasted at Leningrad and in Tunisia thanks to the Führer's impatience. He was very vocal in his post-war criticism of Hitler's treatment of the Tiger. In North Africa they became an issue of contention between Generals Irwin Rommel and von Arnim in the dying days of the Nazi foothold in Tunisia.

It is notable that Field Marshal Erich von Manstein, in his memoirs *Lost Victories* and General Reinhard Gehlen, in *The Gehlen Memoirs*, make no mention of the Tiger's role or impact at Kursk – the Nazis' last major offensive on the Eastern Front. If anyone were to sing its praises, it would have been Manstein, who commanded Army Group South with such incredible flair, and Gehlen, who was in charge of intelligence on the Eastern Front. As far as they were concerned, it was just another panzer. Ultimately, they had much bigger strategic axes to grind.

Panzer Corps commander General von Mellenthin was complimentary about the Tiger's role at Kursk: 'the spearhead of the wedge was formed by the heaviest tanks, and the Tigers proved their worth against the Russian anti-tank fronts organised in depth'. While the Tiger may have done sterling work, the reality was that it was unable to cut through the Soviet defences completely or help stave off Hitler's inevitable defeat at Kursk. Instead, it was compelled to cover the German retreat.

Ultimately, it was the handful of extremely tough German tank aces, such as Johannes Bölter, Otto Carius, Kurt Knispel, Martin Schroif and Michael Wittmann, who achieved incredible success with the Tiger against remarkable odds, that really sealed the tank's all-pervading reputation. The likes of Michael Wittmann, fearlessly knocking out enemy tank after enemy tank, erroneously convinced many Allied tankers that the Tiger was all but invincible. Wittmann's eventual death in action clearly signalled that this was not the case.

Since then, as well as military historians, Hollywood has had an on/off infatuation with the Tiger. The most notable movies are *Saving Private Ryan*, *Kelly's Heroes*, *Night of the Generals* and the lesser known *The Battle of Neretva*, all of which feature passable replicas. Enthusiasts will argue that these are not 'real' Tigers, but nonetheless the filmmakers made a good job using available materials. This is especially the case when you consider that over the years American M26s, M47s and German Leopards have all been called upon to masquerade – often unconvincingly – as Tiger tanks in various movies. The Russians even built a high-quality functioning replica for the film *White Tiger*. Very few original Tigers remain and only one of those has been restored to running order.

It should be highlighted that, although this book is part of the highly successful and well-established Images of War series, Pen & Sword felt that in light of the subject matter's fame it warranted a slightly different approach. To that end the publisher has commissioned a series of colour illustrations that show the major variants of the Tiger in close detail. It was also felt, in light of reader feedback, that the text should be longer than usual in order to offer a much more in-depth exploration and analysis of the history of the tank, and consequently fewer photographs have been included than in some of the other volumes in the series.

Photograph Sources

The photos in this book are drawn from the Canadian National Archives, US Army Archive sources, Cobbaton Combat Collection and the Scott Pick Collection, as well as the author's own collection. Notably, Cobbaton has one of the very few remaining examples of the British towed 17-pounder anti-tank gun, which proved the nemesis of the Tiger tank. The author is grateful to Preston Isaac for the images of the museum's restored weapon.

The author would also like to thank Jean Norman for sharing her late husband Alf's photos. He served through the 1944–45 Northwest Europe campaign as a gunner with the 83rd Field Regiment, Royal Artillery, 53rd (Welsh) Division, and his service documents include some interesting shots of the Tiger. Inevitably the quality of the images varies greatly, and some poorer-quality ones have been included for their novelty or uniqueness.

Prologue: Peashooters Against Behemoths

The crane's gantry groaned under the weight of the 60-ton panzer, the pulleys and cables creaking as the operator gently swung the vehicle from the freighter's cargo hold onto the quayside at Bizerte, Tunisia. The crane operator was an experienced hand but now was no time to be making silly mistakes – this tank was well travelled, having come all the way from the industrial city of Kassel on the Fulda River in central Germany.

Mechanics clambered on to the vehicle and prepared to make it roadworthy after its sea journey. Although it was winter, the weather was much milder than back home. It was certainly warmer than the hated Eastern Front and the men laboured in their shirtsleeves.

Finally, when the tank was pronounced ready, the Panzertruppen climbed on board. The driver's head peeped out just above the hull. The massive V12 Maybach engine roared into life and the exhausts belched a cloud of choking black fumes. The tank, a symbol of Nazi engineering excellence, rumbled along the quay – and promptly broke down. This embarrassing mishap marked the Tiger tank's entry into the war in North Africa. All this, though, would soon change.

The inexperienced US Army was having a bad day; the Germans had caught them on the hop again in Tunisia. Only months earlier US tankers had cut their teeth against ropey old light tanks belonging to the Vichy French armed forces and thankfully the fight had gone their way. Now they were facing a surprise attack by battle-hardened panzers and were on the receiving end of the German mantra 'attack is the best form of defence.'

American positions had been overrun by the panzers and they were now counterattacking with elements of the US 1st Armoured Division. The unit charging into battle was equipped with the Stuart light tank, affectionately dubbed the 'Honey' by a grateful British Army; fast and reliable, the Stuart was a vast improvement on the British Mark VI light tank. The only drawback was that it was armed with a 37mm gun and this was being pitted against the invulnerable armour of the PzKpfw VI Ausf E – better known as the Tiger tank.

The Yanks certainly had guts. As the only unit available to try to stem the German tide, they roared into action. However, their guns were little better than peashooters and they resorted to trying to take out the panzers' optics. The American crews began firing as quickly and accurately as they could. The boom of their guns was rapidly followed by the dull clank of their shells impacting to no effect on the enemy's thick armour. It was 'like peas off a tin pot,' said one 37mm gunner. In fact, the 37mm gun had little chance of penetrating any panzer, even at minimum range. Such aggression, though, could not go unanswered, or indeed unpunished.

The Stuarts were torn apart in the uneven struggle, the Tiger's vast 88mm gun chewing up men and armour with alarming ease. When the American M4 Sherman tank joined the battle, the outcome was the same. The US Army was gripped with a sense of panic. Defeat seemed inevitable — and so was born the legend of the invincible Tiger.

Chapter One

Tiger I:
Henschel or Porsche?

The evolution of the Tiger I is a story of lost opportunities, both in design terms and operationally. By the spring of 1941, following the Wehrmacht's experiences fighting the British Matilda and French Char B heavy tanks, Adolf Hitler was firmly of the view that he needed a tank heavier than his existing Panzer Mk IV. Although work had been carried out in the late 1930s on producing a successor to the Panzer Mk III and IV, the designs had come to nothing. The development of the Tiger I was tortuous, going through at least six different design stages.

In 1937 the Waffenamt (German Ordnance Department) tasked Henschel with developing a heavy breakthrough tank that would be twice the weight of the Panzer IV. The first prototype, dubbed the DW I (Henschel Durchbruchwagen – 'breakthrough vehicle') was completed in September 1938; it had five road wheels and was sprung by torsion bars, while the side armour comprised two pieces joined at the back of the fighting compartment.

Despite the fact that war was looming over Europe, the DW I trials were suspended to allow work on a huge 65-ton tank designated the VK 6501. VK was short for Vollkettenkraftfahrzeug, or 'fully tracked experimental vehicle 65 tons, first design'. Two VK 6501 prototypes were built, only for work to be switched back to the DW I.

The follow-on DW II appeared in 1940, featuring one-piece side armour and different tracks. The engine, a Maybach HL 120 coupled to a Maybach Variorex eight-speed gearbox, gave a speed of 35km/hr. Weighing in at 32 tons, it had a crew of five and was to have been armed with the short 75mm gun used on the Panzer IV. Lacking any apparent sense of urgency, this work now lapsed, though the hull arrangement would be used on the VK 3001(H).

The VK 3001 project was authorised by the Waffenamt on 9 September 1938. Henschel turned to the DW II but replaced the needle-bearing tracks with dry-pin tracks. However, trials did not take place until early 1940, when eight test vehicles were ordered. The first VK 3001 did not appear until March 1941, and two months later it was decided to go with the heavier 36-ton VK 3601 requirement. Subsequently two further VK 3001(H) examples were finished, along with twelve turrets built by Krupp.

While Henschel was working on the VK 3001 design, the Porsche design bureau was conducting similar research. Although officially designated the VK 3001(P), Porsche designers knew it as the Type 100 or the Leopard. For the suspension Dr Ferdinand Porsche employed longitudinal torsion bars mounted externally, while power was supplied by air-cooled engines and electric transmission. Two prototypes were produced between 1940 and 1941, but the engines proved problematical and they went the way of the Henschel prototypes.

These plans, though, had to be resurrected in the summer of 1941 when it was discovered that Soviet tank design had stolen a march on the Germans with the T-34 and KV-1, in terms of both armour and firepower. The initial remit was to procure a tank mounting a gun capable of piercing 100mm of armour at 1,500 metres. At the same time, the design had to be able to take similar punishment. Hitler turned to Henschel and Porsche once more. It is quite remarkable that Hitler, who had already committed Nazi Germany to fighting a two-front war, felt he had time to indulge in developing two competing designs. To complicate matters further, Krupp received the contract to produce turrets for both the Henschel and Porsche designs.

Henschel was requested to design a tank in the range of 36–40 tons armed with a tapered squeeze bore gun (designated Waffen 0725) to be produced under Project VK 3601, while under Project VK 4501 Porsche was asked to come up with a 45-ton vehicle capable of taking an anti-tank version of the 88mm flak gun.

Once again the staff at Henschel found themselves going down a blind alley. Although drawing on the VK 3001(H), the VK 3601(H) had larger road wheels on eight axles. The lack of adequate foresight immediately stymied the Waffen 0725: because of the war tungsten steel was in short supply, which meant ammunition for the tapered bore guns could not be produced. Hitler cancelled Waffen 0725 and opted to use the VK 4501 turret on the 3601. This in turn caused further problems because the replacement turret had a larger diameter, meaning the hull superstructure had to be widened to accommodate it. The knock-on effect of increasing the superstructure and the track width caused a weight increase that required an extra run of road wheels to decrease ground pressure. This became Project VK 4501(H).

Henschel's designers were able to draw on the key features of their VK 3001(H) and VK 3601(H) programmes, though they must have despaired at the ever-changing requirements each time the specification was revised and the tank became heavier.

A side view of an early production Tiger I. Note the cylindrical cupola with vision slits, the machine-pistol port at the rear of the turret by the storage bin, and the distinctive rubber-rimmed dish-shaped road wheels.

They built two models, the H1, mounting an 88mm KwK 36 L/56 gun, and the H2, with a 75mm KwK L/70 gun in a Porsche turret. In practice, the H2 only got as far as a wooden mock-up. To avoid confusion the Porsche H1 was redesignated the VK 4501 (P), and it drew on the earlier, cancelled, VK 3001 (P). However, the Porsche air-cooled engines essentially did not work, forcing Porsche to consider abandoning electric transmission for a hydraulic one.

Both the Henschel and Porsche prototypes were put through their paces before Hitler at Rastenburg on his birthday on 20 April 1942. It soon became apparent that the Henschel design was much more ready for mass production, with far fewer teething problems. Not only did the Porsche lose out, but also its name was appropriated by the Henschel vehicle and thus the PzKpfw VI Tiger was born. Judged a far superior design by virtue of its conventional layout and construction methods, the Henschel tank was officially designated the Panzerkampfwagen VI Tiger Ausf H, and its Sonderkraftfahrzeug (ordnance number) was Sd Kfz 181. However, in February 1944 its designation was altered to PzKpfw Tiger Ausf E, Sd Kfz 181.

The Henschel Tiger had eight sets of triple overlapping and interleaved road wheels with a torsion bar suspension to give optimum distribution of its 57-ton weight. The superstructure and the hull were welded together, with the superstructure extending out over the tracks to allow for the wider turret. The 88mm KwK 36 was fitted coaxially with an MG34 machine gun in the external gun mantlet.

Another early production Tiger captured in Tunisia by the US Army; a GI occupies its cupola with forward-opening hatch.

Despite a lack of preliminary testing, Porsche Tiger production had been instigated with delivery scheduled for July 1942. Problems with the V10 air-cooled engines and the suspension meant only five had been built when production came to a halt in August 1942. As the Porsche Tigers had air-cooled engines, the intention had been to form two detachments for service in North Africa, but instead the completed vehicles were sent to Döllersheim for training purposes. Production was officially abandoned because Porsche proved unable to resolve the technical difficulties.

Although only a single model Henschel Tiger I was produced, there were a number of distinctive changes during the vehicle's production life. The initial Tiger Is are identifiable by their rubber-rimmed road wheels, the large Feifel air cleaners at the rear, the tall commander's cupola and dual headlights. While the mid-production Tiger I retained the rubber-rimmed road wheels, it has a different turret that included a smaller cupola. Finally the late production Tiger I from January 1944 is instantly recognisable by its all-steel disc wheels, which were internally sprung, and its periscope-equipped cupola.

It was soon found that the selected Maybach V-12 petrol engine, the 21-litre HL 210 P45, was just too underpowered and from December 1943 it was replaced by the 24-litre HL 230 P45. The sheer weight of the Tiger made the use of the earlier clutch and brake type of steering impractical. Instead, Henschel produced something similar to the British Merritt-Brown steering unit that was regenerative and continuous. The gearbox provided eight forward gear ratios and allowed for a twin radius of turn in each gear. This and the pre-selector made the Tiger relatively easy to handle, despite its size.

Nonetheless the Tiger's overall lack of mobility and relatively low speed meant it was vulnerable to flank attack. The Germans compensated for this by adding platoons of Panzer IIIs or IVs to the Tiger battalions to act as flank guards. These flanking platoons usually had the thankless task of moving forward first, which inevitably meant they also acted as decoys, drawing enemy fire; then the Tigers, using their longer-range guns, could zero in on the enemy and pick them off. The other job of the Panzer IIIs and IVs was of course to cover the Tigers' withdrawal if they were forced to retreat.

To avoid joins and welds, the Tiger I's turret was made from a single plate bent into a horseshoe shape. Initially this had a cylindrical cupola with vision slits and two machine pistol ports in the rear. An escape hatch replaced the right-hand pistol port in December 1942 and the cupola was replaced by a design incorporating periscopes in July 1943. While the specified weight of 45 tons was exceeded by up to 11 tons with the production models, when the Tiger entered the war in late 1942 it was the best armed and most heavily armoured tank in existence.

The famous 88mm flak gun provided the basis of the Tiger's powerful anti-tank gun.

The Tiger's main armament was the 88mm KwK 36 anti-tank gun that had ballistic qualities similar to the famous Flak 18 and Flak 36 88mm anti-aircraft guns from which it was derived. Modifications included a muzzle brake and electric firing by a trigger-operated primer on the elevating hand wheel. In addition, a 7.92mm MG34 was coaxially mounted on the left side of the 88mm, which was fired by a foot pedal operated by the gunner.

The KwK 36's breech was of the semi-automatic falling wedge type, but scaled up. The weight of the barrel was counterbalanced through a large coil spring housed in a cylinder on the left front of the turret. The elevation and hand traverse were operated by the gunner by hand wheels to his right and left respectively. The commander also had an emergency traverse hand wheel. The gunner also operated the hydraulic power traverse by rocking a right hand footplate. Due to its weight, the turret had to be rotated in low gear. To do this manually took the gunner 720 turns of the hand wheel to get a full 360 rotation. Likewise a power traverse through 180 degrees required a lot of footwork and concentration. This delay often meant that Allied tanks were able to get off the first shot – though it was often their last.

The gunner was provided with a binocular telescope for sighting the 88mm gun, a clinometer for firing high explosive and a turret position indicator dial. As space was at a premium, the main gun ammunition was stored on either side of the fighting compartment and partly alongside the driver in storage bins, as well as under the turret floor.

(*Above*) This early production Tiger was photographed on the Eastern Front. It appears to have been whitewashed, though the road wheels remain their original colour.

(*Opposite, top*) Another initial production model undergoing gunnery practice on the Eastern Front. The bulky Feifel system can be seen on the left just above the tracks.

(*Opposite, below*) This mid-production Tiger I was abandoned in Normandy in 1944. It retained the rubber-rimmed road wheels but had a smaller cupola with periscopes. The air cleaning system had been dispensed with by this stage.

British or Canadian troops examining a late production Tiger, identifiable by its steel road wheels, in Normandy. This particular vehicle has lost its track guards.

As the overall weight of the production Tiger was simply too great for most bridges, it was decided to give it a wading and submersion capability. The first 495 tanks were equipped for snorkel breathing and could cope in water up to 13ft deep. This required all the doors and hatches to be fitted with rubber seals, while the turret ring was waterproofed using an inflatable rubber tube. Likewise the gun mantlet was fitted with a sliding frame with a sealing ring, while the machine-gun ports were bunged using expanding rubber plugs once the machine guns had been removed. Air for the engine and the crew came in via a snorkel pipe. In theory the Tiger could stay under water for up to two and half hours, but all this equipment was highly expensive and time-consuming to fit. Inevitably, as economies had to be made, this was abandoned, leaving the Tiger capable of tackling depths of only 4ft.

Early Tigers were also equipped with a particularly gruesome, if not ingenious, anti-personnel defence system. This was the 'S' mine: an anti-personnel bomb about 4in wide and 5in deep. This exploded at up to 5ft in the air, blasting the immediate area with 360 [³/₈]-in steel balls, thereby killing any enemy infantry threatening the tank. The mine dischargers were fitted to the superstructure, with a total of five being mounted in various positions.

To simplify construction, the Tiger's hull sections and superstructure were welded rather than bolted together. The front and rear of the superstructure consisted of one unit, and interlocking stepped joints, fixed by welding, were used for both the superstructure and the lower hull. Side panniers were created by extending the superstructure out over the tracks and to the full length of the hull. The top front plate of the hull covered the full width of the tank, and it was this width that allowed for an internal diameter turret ring of 6ft 1in that housed the breech and mounting of the 88mm gun. The breech mechanism almost reached the inside rear turret wall, effectively dividing the fighting compartment in two.

Inside, the hull was divided into four compartments: two forward compartments housing the driver and bow gunner/wireless operator, a central fighting compartment and the rear engine compartment. The driver sat to the left, steering via a wheel that acted hydraulically on the tank's controlled differential steering unit. The driver's visor was opened and closed using a sliding shutter operated by a hand wheel on the front vertical plate. Periscopes were fitted on both the driver's and wireless operator's escape hatches.

Another late production model getting the once-over in Normandy. The corrugated surface on this tank (and the previous one) is due to the Zimmerit paste that was applied from 1943 onwards to prevent the attaching of magnetic anti-tank hollow charges.

(*Above*) This late model is likewise a source of fascination for British troops.

(*Opposite, top*) Although the Red Army stole a march over the Germans in developing heavy tanks, their T-35, KV-1 and KV-2 (seen here) models proved unsuccessful.

(*Opposite, below*) The Soviet T-35 heavy tank proved an ungainly disaster.

A good view of the much flatter steel wheels on the late production Tiger. This tank has seen some rough going, judging by the track guards and the bent wheels.

Early and mid-production Tigers being shipped to the front.

This mid-production Tiger is fitted with its narrow road tracks, to accommodate which the outer row of road wheels has been removed and stacked behind the tank.

An early Tiger negotiating a log road. Despite the wide off-road tracks, the tank's weight could be a problem on soft ground.

An early Tiger training in a hull-down position, which proved highly effective in Normandy.

It was the Tiger I's armour that made it such a tough nut to crack. The contemporary model of the Panzer IV Ausf G and Panzer III Ausf L/M and N had only 50mm of armour on the front of the turret, superstructure and hull (though they were given additional 20mm spaced armour), and 30mm on the sides. The Tiger I sported much stronger armour, with 100mm on the front, 60mm on the sides and 80mm at the rear. The top and bottom armour was 25mm thick, with the turret roof thickened to 40mm in March 1944.

Initially production was planned to commence in July 1942, with 285 ready by May 1943 in time for Hitler's major summer offensive on the Eastern Front. Once the Porsche Tiger contract had been halted, the Henschel order was increased by fifty to make up the shortfall. Production commenced in August 1942 at a rate of just twelve tanks per month. By November this had been increased to twenty-five per month. Maximum production was reached in April 1944 when 104 Tigers rolled off the assembly lines.

The Tiger I and the subsequent Tiger II were particularly vulnerable to the Allied bomber offensive, as only one factory was involved in producing them. Tiger I production ran from July 1942 until August 1944, and Tiger II production from January 1944 to March 1945. Henschel achieved a monthly rate of 106 Tigers in the summer of 1944, but this had dropped to just thirty-six by the autumn. By early December 1944 these attacks and the general disruption caused by the strategic bombing campaign had cost the Germans at least 200 Tigers.

Chapter Two

Tiger II's Troubled Birth

Hitler's second heavy tank, the Tiger II, was one of the largest and most impressive panzers ever built. Armour- and armament-wise, it was formidable, and this, combined with its distinctive appearance, made it a particularly terrifying tank to come up against. However, its weight and mobility were another matter and, as with the Tiger I, these handicaps and its limited production run proved to be its undoing.

Although dubbed the Tiger II, this heavy tank was in fact a new design that in appearance at least had more in common with the Panther than with the Tiger I. The last German heavy tank, it was known variously as the Tiger Ausf B, Tiger II or King Tiger (Königstiger), while the Western Allies dubbed it rather grandly the Royal Tiger. Its ordnance inventory number was Sd Kfz 182. For the purposes of this book, and for the sake of consistency, we will use the term Tiger II.

The requirement for the Tiger II originated in the summer of 1942, when the German Ordnance Department issued specifications for a Tiger I replacement that would be superior to the T-34 in terms of both firepower and armour. Both Henschel and MAN, which built the Panther, were asked to design second-generation vehicles for the Tiger and the Panther respectively. Porsche was also asked to meet the replacement Tiger requirement with VK 4502. Rather than start from scratch, Porsche adapted his earlier unsuccessful Tiger designs.

The Porsche design offered two different layouts, with the turret mounted either at the front or the back of the hull. The latter had sloped armour similar to that of the Panther. Like the previous Porsche projects, the suspension had paired bogies with longitudinal torsion bars. Wegmann designed the turret to take the 88mm KwK 43 L/71 gun and fifty were ordered, but VK 4502(P) was abandoned. Porsche's final submission was hampered by the retention of the ill-fated petrol-electric drive, plus the scarcity of the copper needed for the transmission.

VK 4502(H) was also rejected, so Henschel submitted the revised VK 4503(H). This design, although based on the original Tiger concept, had to be considerably modified because of the Ordnance Department's insistence that it must incorporate most of the features included in the Panther II programme. Not unreasonably, the

The massive Tiger II had more in common with the Panther in terms of shape. This model has the improved turret that eliminated the shot trap. It's coated in Zimmerit, factory painted in dunkel gelb and then sprayed in patches of olivgrun across the hull, turret and barrel.

Ordnance Department was trying to achieve commonality in spare parts for these projected new tanks. While this was accepted, the design work was not completed until 1943. The MAN project VK 5402(MAN) was accepted, but the war ended before the Panther II could go into production.

Attempts to enhance the Tiger I by replacing the KwK 36 L/56 88mm anti-tank gun with the improved KwK 43 L/71 were thwarted by the lack of space in the turret. In January 1943 Hitler ordered that the new Tiger must have a turret large enough to mount the L/71. Also, the frontal armour was to increase to 150mm, though the sides were to remain at 80mm. To this end Henschel displayed an enormous wooden mock-up on 20 October 1943 to give Hitler some idea of the size of the new vehicle. Initially the VK 4502(P) turret, with a distinctive curved front and curved mantlet, was selected to house the L/71, though in reality this turret was designed with both prototypes in mind.

By November 1943 the Henschel Tiger II pilot model was ready and production commenced at the Henschel factory in Kassel in December 1943, with the first models completed by February 1944. In total, only about 500 Tiger IIs were built by the end of the war. Under the rationalisation programme of autumn 1944, according to which only two tanks with traversing turrets would be produced in 1945, the Panther Ausf G and Tiger II were chosen. However, two Panthers could be produced for every Tiger. Production of the Tiger II was scheduled at twenty a month, ramping

This knocked-out Tiger II also has the newer turret design.

British troops examining a Tiger II in France with the initial rounded Porsche turret that has been blown off the chassis.

up to 145. In reality, the highest it reached was eighty-four in the summer of 1944, with the number falling to just twenty-five in March 1945.

There were grandiose plans to build 1,500 Tiger IIs, but the Allied bomber offensive put paid to that. Between 22 September and 7 October 1944 five raids took out 95 per cent of the Henschel factory floor at Kassel. This cost the loss of production of almost 660 Tiger IIs. As a result, one was produced in 1943, 379 in 1944 and 112 in 1945 giving a total of 492 tanks. By that stage the Tiger II was the best protected mass-produced tank. Its hull armour was up to 150mm thick on the glacis plate at 40 degrees, while the nose was shielded by 100mm at 55 degrees. The turret and hull had armour of 80mm, while the top and belly plates were 42mm thick.

The first fifty Tiger IIs were fitted with the Wegmann turrets that had been built for the abandoned VK 4502(P). The curved front to the turret was soon found to create an unwelcome shot trap. On 6 December 1943 this feature was ordered to

A Tiger II in a bomb crater in Normandy; the turret was torn off in the blast that destroyed it.

Another Tiger II with the Porsche turret abandoned at the roadside in Normandy.

be removed and Henschel quickly redesigned the gun mantlet and the front of the turret to eliminate the curve. They did this by decreasing the frontal area of the turret and installing a bell-shaped mantlet.

Internally the Tiger II layout was almost the same as the Panther, though there was no turret basket. While externally the Tiger II shared some of the heritage of the Panther's sloping body work, some of its design features came from the Tiger I. For example, the engine, engine covers and cupola were common to the Tiger I, as well as to the later Panther. In addition, the all-steel resilient wheels were common to the late production Tiger I and the very late production Panther Ausf G.

The massive suspension system comprised torsion bars with nine sets of overlapped wheels, rather than interleaved wheels as on the Tiger I and Panther. This cut down on clogging and made wheel changes easier. While the wheels were all steel, they had resilient rubber cushions and this cut down on tyre rubber. The tracks came in narrow and wide versions, as on the Tiger I.

The Tiger II was armed with the massive 88mm L/71, an improved and longer version of the gun used in the Tiger I. To allow for instant firing, twenty-two rounds were stored in racks in the rear of the turret with the tips of the rounds facing the breech mechanism. The gun had a monocular sight, while the commander had the advantage of a vision cupola identical to that used in the later model Panther.

The Tiger II could kill all Allied tanks head-on at a range of over 2.5km, easily outreaching Allied tank guns. Indeed, until the arrival of the American M26 Pershing armed with a 90mm gun in February 1945, neither the British nor the Americans had any heavy tanks. The only Allied gun capable of tackling the Tiger at around 1,100 metres was the British 17-pounder installed in the Sherman Firefly.

The Tiger II's Achilles heel, as with all panzers, was its underpowered gasoline engine. Although the Tiger II weighed almost 70 tonnes, it had the same engine as the much lighter Tiger I and Panther, namely the V12 Maybach HL 230 P30. There were plans to upgrade the engine with the inclusion of fuel injection and an up-rated drivetrain, but this never happened. Likewise, there was talk of replacing the main gun with a 105mm KwK L/68.

Initially the Tiger II suffered from an overburdened drivetrain, while the double radius steering gear had a nasty habit of failing and the gaskets and seals leaked. The Tiger IIs delivered to Heavy Panzer Battalion 501 almost all suffered from drivetrain failures, which meant that when the unit arrived on the Eastern Front only eight of its forty-five tanks were operational. Similarly the first five Tiger IIs sent to the Panzer Lehr Division broke down and had to be destroyed to prevent their capture before

The rear of the same tank.

(*Above*) A frontal view showing the curve of the Porsche turret. The tank in front of it is a Bergepanther recovery vehicle.

(*Opposite*) Two views of a Tiger II knocked out during the Ardennes offensive. Note the distinctive camouflage applied to the hull, track guards and turret. Track links have been placed on the turret to enhance the armour.

they had even seen any action. Modifications to the Tiger II greatly improved its reliability, but by that stage the war was coming to a close.

Despite the tank's massive size, it offered good visibility. The driver was equipped with a periscope in the roof of the hull and he could raise the seat if he was driving with his hatch open. Also an episcope provided vision for the hull machine gunner, while there was another one in the turret roof for the gunner.

The Tiger II was issued to the training units in February and May 1944, but did not reach the first combat units until June, some five months after production had commenced. They were all issued to the independent heavy panzer battalions except for five, which were sent to the Feldherrnhalle Division in March 1945.

In a head-to-head shoot-out, the Tiger II outranged almost all Allied tanks and was practically impervious to all Allied armoured-piercing rounds. However, as with the Tiger I, there were simply too few Tiger IIs. And while it was well armoured and armed, it was still an unwieldy tank. Like its predecessor, its weight and size made it a tactical liability. It was simply too heavy for most road bridges and it offered a large target for enemy gunners and fighter-bombers. The Tiger IIs' finest moment came during Hitler's Ardennes offensive, when it was partnered with the Panther. Its subsequent role in Hitler's counteroffensive in Hungary, however, only proved what a liability it was.

Like all panzers manufactured in the later part of the war, the Tiger II suffered from quality control problems. Inevitably the lack of alloys impacted on the steel. This meant that when the armour was hit, even if the round did not penetrate, the welds quite often cracked and there was extensive spalling. The latter could be dangerous to the crews if this occurred on the inside.

In the summer of 1944 the Red Army fighting at Sandomierz captured a number of Tiger IIs, which were whisked off to the Soviet tank-testing ground at Kubinka. The Soviets were not impressed with what they found. The underpowered engine overheated and packed up, and the transmission and suspension regularly gave out. Anti-tank gun tests showed how shoddy the armour was. The quality of the welding was found to be very poor and welds tended to crack after repeated battering by anti-tank shells.

Colour Schemes

One question that needs addressing is what colour the Tigers were painted. A popular misconception among the public, thanks largely to Hollywood, is that all German military vehicles were a dull panzer grey. Certainly from 1939 German Army vehicles were painted dunkel grau, generally known as panzer grey. This was intended to help vehicle outlines merge with buildings and trees in Western Europe. The national identification mark for all German vehicles was a black cross edged in white, with all unit signs and arm of service symbols also in white. Tactical numbers varied in colour but were again normally edged in white.

This snow-covered tank was also lost during the Ardennes offensive.

The fighting in North Africa led to the introduction of gelb braun (brownish yellow) in early 1941. Once the German Army had invaded Russia, dunkel grau served very little purpose on the open steppes and it was discontinued in early 1943. From mid-February 1943 the German Army standardised its basic vehicle colour as dunkel gelb (a deep sand yellow). All vehicles coming out of the factories were sprayed in this colour, with the paint applied over the Zimmerit anti-magnetic paste, which gave the surface of the tanks a corrugated appearance. However, much of the old equipment remained panzer grey, particularly that used by occupation and reserve forces. There has been some debate over whether dunkel grau was reintroduced for front-line armour in 1944, but this seems to have arisen from some of the test vehicles at such places as Henschel being panzer grey.

The basic colour for all German armour in Northwest Europe was entirely dunkel gelb. Combat conditions at the front meant that few crews had the time or inclination to ensure that their vehicles conformed to official dictates. A new camouflage pattern was also introduced in February 1943 which employed two other colours, olivgrun (olive green) and rotbraun (reddish brown). Again the net result was that vehicles ended up painted in what best suited their immediate field conditions. The patterns varied enormously, with dappling and zigzagging, spots, stripes and splinter patterns. Nonetheless some elite formations such as the SS and Tiger II detachments made attempts at uniformity.

Each vehicle was issued tins of dunkel gelb, olivgrun and rotbraun. Photographic evidence suggests that the latter was used the most, and it certainly helped when

A Tiger II in Osterode, Germany, April 1945. A well-aimed Bazooka round pierced the turret on the left-hand side.

fighting in built-up areas. The coverage and consistency of the paint varied enormously as the three colours were issued as a very thick paste that could be diluted with water or petrol (though the latter was a commodity that could rarely be spared for thinning paint). This meant that the tone and colour of the paint varied from vehicle to vehicle. It also meant that tanks within a single unit could end up with both dark and light shades – the green could range from pea green to black, while the brown could be a light brick red to a deep maroon. Using water to dilute the paste had the drawback that the colour was not durable and tended to wash off in even the lightest of rain. By the end of the war many vehicles were deployed in just their factory-finish dunkel gelb as there was no time to add any disruptive camouflage. Jagdtigers were captured with such a finish.

Application of the paint also gave differing results. In theory, each tank was issued with a small spray gun and compressor run off the vehicle's engine. Crews given the choice of slapping it on with a broom, paintbrush and rag, or mucking about with a spray gun, normally opted for the former when in the field. When the workshops had time to do a proper spray job the olivgrun ended up dark green and the rotbraun a deep chocolate colour. Add in dirt, dust, mud, oil and petrol and camouflage schemes soon became very grubby and blurred. Certainly on the Eastern Front mud was deliberately used as a natural camouflage. In November 1941 the German Army introduced a washable white paint for use on the Eastern Front during the winter, and it was also used in Northwest Europe during the winter of 1944/45. In the case of the latter, a Tiger I was photographed in overall dunkel gelb with snow camouflage added by daubing thick white paint in irregular patches on the hull and turret.

In Tunisia the Tigers had a base colour of dunkel gelb. Likewise those initially deployed to Russia were largely sand yellow with varying degrees of camouflage or whitewash depending on the time of year. Tiger Is fighting with the 1st SS Panzer Division in Normandy in the summer of 1944 had their overall dunkel gelb broken up by being sprayed with a pattern in olivgrun. For the sake of speed, the wheels usually remained dunkel gelb, while the barrel was mainly olivgrun with insignia restricted to the national identification mark.

The Tiger IIs in Normandy had a three-colour scheme comprising dunkel gelb, olivgrun and rotbraun. The tactical number and cross were in black edged with white. A large number of panzers did not make use of snow camouflage during the Ardennes offensive. This was especially the case with the Tiger IIs committed to the battle, which sported the standard late war tri-colour panzer camouflage scheme. The Tiger IIs with SS Heavy Panzer Battalion 501 were painted in an 'ambush scheme' that included spots presumably added by paintbrush. This is clearly visible on the Tondorf film footage of the unit. For further guidance, see colour plates.

Chapter Three

Tiger I and II Variants

Tiger I Command Panzer

Two command or radio-tank variants of the Tiger I were produced, designated the Panzerbefehlswagen VI Ausf E Sd Kfz 267 and the Sd Kfz 268. They carried additional radio sets (the FunkSprechGerät 8 and FunkSprechGerät 7 respectively) that enabled the commander to communicate at divisional level and ground to air. The extra space taken up by the radios meant a reduction in the number of rounds normally carried from ninety-two to sixty-six, and also resulted in a slight reduction in the amount of machine-gun ammunition. Just eighty-four of these command tanks were produced in 1944 and they were all but indistinguishable from the regular Tiger I. The only give-away was the addition of a turret-mounted radio aerial (the aerial for the tactical radio was on the rear right-hand side of the hull).

Tiger I Recovery Panzer

The weight of the Tiger I meant that recovering disabled tanks was a major problem. In 1944 three Tiger I Ausf E were reportedly converted to Bergepanzers by removing the main gun, installing a winch inside the turret and fitting a small tubular crane to the front of the turret and a geared winch mount to the rear. These were ad hoc battlefield conversions and in one instance the turret was also fitted with the Panther-type commander's cupola with seven episcopes and an anti-aircraft gun mounting ring.

   One of these Bergepanzer Tigers was captured on a roadside in Italy in 1944. Subsequent examination has shown that the crane was in fact far too light to be used for towing broken-down panzers. It has since been postulated that this was in fact not a recovery tank at all, but an engineer vehicle used for depositing explosives to destroy battlefield obstacles or as some sort of mine-clearing vehicle.

Tiger I Sturmtiger

Among the many specialised types of armoured fighting vehicles developed for the German Army was the Sturmpanzer (assault tank). The best known is the 'Grizzly Bear' Sturmpanzer IV Brummbar, which was developed to help in the street-fighting

The formidable-looking Sturmtiger was designed to smash Soviet strongpoints and buildings, but by the time it came into service this requirement had long passed.

in the Soviet Union's cities. Even more formidable was the Sturmtiger, also known as the Sturmpanzer VI or Sturmmörser. This vehicle arose from the Germans' experiences fighting in the city of Stalingrad, where they decided they needed a weapon that could destroy a strongpoint with a single shot. Its full designation was the 380mm RW 61 Auf StuMrs Tiger; Hitler's brainchild, it consisted of a 380mm rocket projector Type 61 on a Tiger chassis.

The design came about due to the need for a self-propelled vehicle that could carry a massive 210mm howitzer. The then new PzKpfw VI Tiger Ausf E chassis was chosen to carry the gun, but no suitable 210mm howitzers were available. Instead, the Raketenwerfer 61 L/54, which was originally produced by the firm Rheinmetall-Borsig as an anti-submarine weapon for the navy, was selected.

On 20 October 1943 a Sturmtiger prototype by Alkett was displayed for the first time and gained approval. It went into very limited production in the summer of 1944 with Brandenburger Eisenwerke manufacturing the superstructure and Alkett converting the chassis and completing the assembly at their Berlin-Spandau plant. Although its weapon was powerful enough to demolish an entire house, by the time the Sturmtiger went into production, this street-fighting requirement was long gone, as the German Army was in headlong retreat on the Eastern Front.

The suspension, power train, engine and hull were from the basic Tiger Ausf E, but the turret and superstructure had to be replaced with a heavily armoured rectangular body. This was made from welded rolled plates, with the side plates interlocked with the front and rear ones. The joint between the front plate and glacis plate was reinforced with a heavy strip of armour on the outside. The driver's position had the same controls as the Tiger, but the position was much more cramped.

The odd rocket projector (looking more like a drainpipe than a gun) was mounted offset to the right centre in the front of the superstructure. It consisted of a tubular casting with a spaced rifled liner and cast mantlet. The latter was an integral part of the tube and protected the joint of the mount and the tube itself. The gases from the rocket were deflected between the tube and the liner to escape through a perforated ring on the muzzle containing thirty-one holes.

Inside were six ammunition racks capable of holding twelve rounds, either high explosive or hollow charge. The 5ft-long, 761lb high explosive 38mm RaketenSprenggranate 4581 (RS = rocket, self-propelled) rocket had to be loaded into the breech using overhead rails that took a hand-operated winch, which could run from side to side to place the rockets on the loading tray. The rocket was then manhandled from the loading tray, which was fitted with six rollers, into the projector set at zero elevation. The tray was folded into the floor when not in use.

The winch was also used to help with ammunition storage. Reloading the vehicle was just as laborious. A hand-operated small ammunition crane was mounted on the superstructure to lift the rockets from the supply vehicle and lower them through the roof ammunition hatch into the fighting compartment.

Only eighteen existing Tigers were converted during August to December 1944 and were issued to three Sturmmörser (armoured assault) mortar companies, 1001, 1002 and 1003. These were deployed in the defence of the Third Reich and sent to provide fire support for attacks on the advancing Allies. Officially this vehicle had a road speed of 23mph, but with 150mm of frontal armour, 80mm on the sides, 40mm on the roof of the fighting compartment and a gross weight of almost 70 tons, it was highly unmanoeuvrable.

Apart from a few examples serving with an armoured assault mortar company in August 1944 during the Warsaw Rising, the reality is that by this stage of the war the requirement for the Sturmtiger had long gone. Two companies also saw limited service during the Ardennes offensive. Apart from its slowness, the slow rate of fire of the rocket projector rendered the vehicle a positive liability on a highly fluid battlefield. Most of the Sturmtigers would have been abandoned at the first sign of trouble and few ever had the chance of firing in anger. See colour plate 9.

Panzerjäger Tiger (P) Ferdinand/Jagdpanzer Elefant

As part of the Germans' continuing policy of seeking to develop successful tank-killers, the Jagdpanzer (hunting tank) was the next progression from the Sturmgeschütz and panzerjäger, and had the characteristics of both armoured fighting vehicles. A significant example of this was the massive Elefant (initially dubbed the Ferdinand after its designer, Ferdinand Porsche). While it proved to be perhaps the most successful tank destroyer of the war, clocking up a kill ratio of almost 10:1, there were too few of them and they proved to be very unreliable. Ultimately the design was a white elephant.

The original designation was Panzerjäger Tiger (P) Ferdinand für 88mm Pak 43/2, but this was later changed to Jagdpanzer Elefant für 88mm Pak 43/2 L/71 (Sd Kfz 184). To produce a self-propelled mount for the 88mm Pak 43, it was decided that rather than waste the uncompleted Porsche Tigers, which had been rejected in favour of the Henschel design, they would be used as tank-hunters. In addition, the gun was fitted to the Panzer Mk III/IV chassis to create the Nashorn (Rhinoceros), later known as Hornisse (Hornet).

The 88mm Pak 43/2 L/71 anti-tank gun was a development of the earlier 88mm Flak 36 anti-aircraft gun, which was adapted as the weapon of choice for the Tiger. This was a longer and much more powerful weapon than the earlier 88mm L/56. The additional barrel length gave it a greatly increased muzzle velocity and it also

In theory the Ferdinand tank-destroyer was a good use for the rejected Porsche Tiger I chassis.

In reality, the Ferdinand proved vulnerable to Soviet infantry at Kursk. Note the camouflage scheme. This vehicle appears to be partially hull-down and has lost a track.

fired a longer round, which greatly improved its penetration ability. While the Flak 41 became the next generation anti-aircraft gun, the L/71 became the very successful Pak 43 anti-tank gun. The basic design for the Elefant provided no other weapon; this shortcoming soon became a problem and the lack of close protection resulted in the addition of a heavy machine gun at the front of the hull.

In reality, the Elefant was virtually a complete redesign of the original Porsche project. It was really a new vehicle that, despite its lineage, bore little resemblance to the Tiger tank. When the designers had finished, only the hull shape and suspension of the original Porsche Tiger remained.

The Porsche suspension consisted of three twin bogies on each side sprung by torsion bars. The wheels were all steel with resilient rims.

Notably, the original troublesome petrol-electric drive was kept, though in a modified form, with the Porsche air-cooled drive motors replaced by two Maybach 300hp HL 120 engines. These were positioned centrally, rather than in the rear, leaving the rear for the crew fighting compartment. The fuel tanks flanked the engine compartment. The sloped-side fighting compartment housed the commander, gunner and two loaders. At the rear there was a large circular hatch to allow for weapon maintenance, which included a smaller hatch for ejecting spent rounds. There were also two roof hatches and pistol ports.

The driver and radio operator were located in the front of the hull, forward of the engines. Directional control was provided by a hydro-pneumatic steering system. However, visibility was poor and the driver could only see forward, so cupolas had to be added. To enhance crew protection, bolt-on 100mm appliqué armour was added to the nose and 200mm to the front of the superstructure.

The prototype Ferdinand first appeared in March 1943 and ninety-one Porsche Tiger chassis were converted at the Nibelungenwerke factory at St Valentin, Austria, during March to May 1943. For the coming Kursk offensive on the Eastern Front they were issued to the heavy Panzerjäger Battalions 653 and 654 in July 1943 (see colour plate 8). Due to the lack of suitable ammunition transport, six Panzer Mk IIIs were converted into munition Schleppers (carriers).

Panzerjäger Battalions 653 and 654 had both been formed at Bruck the previous April, the 653 raised from personnel of the 197th Sturmgeschütz Battalion. Battalion 653 came under the command of Major Steinwachs and Battalion 654 under Major Karl-Heinz Noak; along with the Brummbars of Sturmpanzer Battalion 216, they formed the 656 Panzerjäger Regiment commanded by Lieutenant Colonel

Even the half-hearted improvements that converted the Ferdinand into the Elefant did little to remedy its shortcomings. This is the rebuilt model with added hull machine gun and commander's cupola.

Jungenfeld. This regiment came under the 41st Panzer Corps, serving with Army Group Centre.

At long range the Ferdinand proved to be deadly and tore great holes in the ranks of Soviet armour. T-34 tanks were reportedly knocked out at a range of over 3 miles. The Ferdinands of Battalion 653 alone knocked out 320 Soviet tanks for the loss of just thirteen of their number, and the regiment as a whole claimed 502 tanks and another 100 vehicles; despite their successes, the Ferdinand's shortcomings rapidly became apparent. Many of them broke down, became stranded or were simply overrun by Russian infantry. After just four days of battle almost half of the eighty-nine Ferdinands committed to the attack were out of service due to technical problems or to mine damage to the tracks and suspension.

Guderian recalled that the Ferdinand's deployment at Kursk was a liability:

the ninety Porsche Tigers, which were operating with Model's Army, were incapable of close-range fighting since they lacked sufficient ammunition for their guns, and this defect was aggravated by the fact that they possessed no machine gun. Once they had broken into the enemy's infantry zone they literally had to go quail shooting with cannons. They did not manage to neutralise, let alone destroy, the enemy rifles and machine guns, so that the infantry was unable to follow up behind them. By the time they reached the Russian artillery they were on their own.

Major Noak's crew had resorted to firing their MG34 machine gun down the barrel of the main armament in a desperate bid to keep the Soviet infantry at bay.

In September the German authorities had little option but to recall the Ferdinand for modification. This included the installation of a much-needed ball-mounted machine gun in the front of the hull, a modified StuG III commander's cupola to help with visibility and a coat of Zimmerit anti-magnetic paste. These modest improvements pushed its weight up from 65 to 70 tons.

The work was again carried out by Nibelungenwerke in Austria and the modernised Ferdinands were perhaps uncharitably dubbed Elefant. This new name became official by order of Hitler on 1 May 1944.

The Elefants were issued to the heavy Panzerjäger Battalion 653 and elements of this unit were shipped to Italy in February 1944. Their weight meant that they were too heavy for most Italian roads and bridges.

The Elefants then saw action at Nettuno, Anzio and Cisterna, but in April 1944 part of the battalion was sent back to the Eastern Front. Then, later in the year, Battalion 653 was re-equipped with Jagdtigers and the remaining Elefants were issued to a new unit, Heavy Panzerjäger Company 614, and resisted the Soviet Army's Vistula-Oder offensive into Poland in January 1945. The last remaining four fought with Battlegroup Ritter south of Berlin in the Zossen area in April 1945.

The rather odd Tiger I 'recovery tank' captured in Italy – it probably had an engineering role rather than a recovery one.

There can be no escaping the fact that the Elefant was a waste of time and effort; it and the Nashhorn were a developmental cul-de-sac. To be fair, the Nashhorn was much more successful, with 473 produced. However you look at it, the Elefant was a rush job with little thought given to its inherent design faults. The reality was that a good gun was married to a very poor vehicle. Essentially the Elefant was a disaster and it was swiftly superseded by much more successful tank-hunters in the shape of the Jagdpanzer IV and the Jagdpanther. Likewise, the Nashhorn was too small, inadequately armoured and underpowered. It too was taken out of production once the much-improved Jagdpanzer types became available.

Bergepanzer Tiger (P)

Three Bergepanzer Tiger (P)s were converted from the Porsche Tiger chassis in September 1943. This was carried out in a similar manner to the Elefant tank-destroyer. The engines were mounted in the centre of the chassis and a new superstructure added at the rear. Apart from a small derrick crane, rams and timber beams, few other concessions were made for its recovery role. A ball-mount was

The formidable Tiger II Jagdtiger proved to be a white elephant owing to reliability problems and the inexperience of its crews.

fitted to the superstructure to give it some defence, using the 7.92mm MG34. Like the Bergepanzer Tiger Ausf E, there were simply too few of them to be of any great help to the panzer crews.

Tiger II Command Panzer
From November 1944 a number of Tiger IIs were converted to Command tanks with the installation of additional radio sets. The command variant of the Tiger II was known as the Panzerbefehlswagen Tiger Ausf B and, like the Tiger I command tanks, it came in two versions, the Sd Kfz 267 and Sd Kfz 268, the former equipped with FuG 5 and FuG 8 radios, and the latter with FuG 5 and FuG 7 radios. These tanks were identifiable by the 2m-long rod antenna mounted on the turret. Accommodating these radios meant they could only carry sixty-three rounds of 88mm ammunition.

Tiger II Jagdtiger
The mighty Jagdtiger was the largest armoured fighting vehicle of the war. A self-propelled adaptation of the Tiger II armed with the enormous 128mm Pak 44 L/55

Two views of the Jagdtiger found in Obernetphen, Germany, in April 1945. The enormous 128mm gun gave the Jagdtiger great killing power but little else.

gun, this was the largest and most powerful anti-tank gun deployed on any wartime fighting vehicle. Weighing in at a whopping 76 tons, it was also the heaviest. The gun, with a muzzle velocity of 2,887ft per second (or 880m/sec), could punch through 143mm of armour at 1,000 yards, meaning it could kill any Allied tank in service.

Initially the use of either the Tiger I or Panther chassis was considered as a possible mount for the 128mm gun, but following the mock-up of a wooden Panther model these designs were abandoned. Likewise, the Krupp Panther Gerät-5 designs for a 105mm, 128mm and 150mm gun carrier all came to nothing.

The limited-traverse tank-hunter version of the Tiger II was produced following Heereswaffenamt policy. Originally designated the Panzerjäger Tiger Ausf B (SdKfz 186), it consisted of the Tiger II hull with a box superstructure to house the gun. A full-size but unarmoured wooden mock-up was ready on 20 October 1943, at the same time as the Tiger II prototype. The finished prototype was not ready until April 1944. In fact, two prototypes were made, one utilising the Henschel suspension system with nine overlapping wheels as used on the Tiger II, and the other the Porsche suspension using eight road wheels.

Attempts were made by Dr Porsche to improve the design with the installation of a torsion bar bogie suspension similar to that used on the prototype Porsche Tiger and the Elefant. Externally it was distinguishable by having one less exterior road wheel on either side (four instead of five). Although Porsche claimed that it greatly simplified production, only a few vehicles ever appeared. Initial intelligence reports suggested that an experimental version fitted with the Porsche suspension was up and running in April 1945, but the war ended before the project could be taken any further. In February 1944 Hitler ordered that the name be simplified and the Panzerjäger Tiger Ausf B (SdKfz 186) officially became the Jagdtiger.

The vital gun mount was a product of joint design work by Henschel and Krupp, and featured a Saukopf mantlet. This offered very limited traverse and elevation, which gave the Jagdtiger a restricted kill zone. The cumbersome box-shaped superstructure to house the gun gave the vehicle a very high and exposed profile. This superstructure was fabricated by Eisenwerke Oberdonau at Linz and was 250mm thick at the front and 80mm thick on the sides.

Like the Tiger II, the Jagdtiger was underpowered, using the V12 Maybach 700hp engine and drivetrain from the late production Tiger I. The driver's station was much more cramped than in the Tiger.

Perhaps not surprisingly, only 150 Panzerjäger Tiger Bs were initially ordered and they were constructed by Steyr-Daimler-Puch at St Valentin in Austria. The war, though, intervened with these modest plans as resources and disruption of the supply chain became an issue.

Early problems with the 128mm gun resulted in proposals to install the 88mm

These Ferdinands were left high and dry during the fighting at Kursk. Like the Jagdtiger, the Ferdinand had a good gun but lacked any other capabilities with which to cope with mobile armoured warfare.

This Ferdinand suffered such a massive internal explosion that its superstructure was torn off the chassis, flipped over and dropped down again.

gun used in the Jagdpanther. A Jagdtiger mounting the 88mm L/71 anti-tank gun (designated the Sd Kfz 185) was designed but never went into production. It is believed that about a dozen of the Sd Kfz 185 variant of the Jagdtiger armed with the 88mm Pak 43 gun were built, though they were never completed due to a lack of components, including sights.

In total, fewer than a hundred Jagdtigers were ever produced. Subsequent factory information indicates that only eleven Jagdtigers were built using the Porsche suspension (eight road wheels) and the rest had the Henschel suspension. Total numbers vary, with reports of forty-eight being built between July and December 1944 and another thirty-six from December 1944 to May 1945. Ultimately this matters little; the fact remains that very few were ever built. In addition, the suspension was the least of its worries as the weight and underpowered engine meant they inevitably kept breaking down.

The Jagdtiger was ideally suited for defensive warfare, with a gun that could destroy every other tank, but its weight and lack of mobility were constant problems for its crews. Its immense size and firepower could not make up for its slow speed and constant breakdowns. The limited numbers of Jagdtigers saw action from late 1944 until the closing days of the war. They were issued to just two combat units, Panzerjägerabteilung 653 and Schwere Panzerabteilung 512. The 653rd saw action on the Western Front during Hitler's Ardennes offensive, and later with the 512th defending the Reich, most notably at the Remagen bridgehead on 10 March 1945.

Two Jagdtigers were captured, in the Morsbronn area of France and near Neustadt in Germany respectively, in March 1945. The former, bearing the number 314, was in the standard dunkel gelb factory colour with a hand-painted pattern of olive green, while the latter had only received its factory base colour. One of the last examples from the 512th Battalion was abandoned on the streets of Obernetphen, Germany, in April 1945. The US 7th Infantry Division captured another serving with the 53rd Panzer Corps at Iserlohn in the Ruhr on 16 April 1945. This Jagdtiger, with the number 102, had a very similar camouflage scheme to the one taken at Morsbronn. Jagdtigers also fell into the hands of the Soviet Army. A battle group from Heavy Panzerjäger Battalion 653, which included four Jagdtigers, surrendered to the Soviets at Amstetten in Austria on 5 May 1945. See colour plate 14.

Chapter Four

Inauspicious Debut

The Tiger crews must have been impressed. This new heavy tank was clearly very different from its predecessors. There was a clear lineage from the Panzer Mark I through to the Mark IV, and they shared very common design features. The Tiger was something else. The first thing that must have struck the panzertruppen was the size of the gun, followed by the shape of the horseshoe turret. Doubtless the Tiger crews would have heard tales from the instructors of how Hitler's Blitzkrieg the previous summer had smashed Stalin's tank fleet, but there was no escaping a sense that the war was becoming bogged down, especially in the face of the bitter Russian winter. The men must have wondered if the Tiger was the weapon with which Hitler hoped to break the deadlock. Indeed, Army Group Centre could have done with it on the road to Moscow.

The appearance of the Soviet T-34 in the summer of 1941 was a cause of vexation to the German High Command. Although the T-34's debut had been unsuccessful, thanks to insufficient numbers and failings in training, tactics and mechanical reliability, if the Soviets were good at one thing it was learning from their mistakes. Above all else, the T-34 was far superior to all the Red Army's previous tanks. Panzer expert General Heinz Guderian called it 'outstanding'.

The T-34's superiority was such that German officers on the Eastern Front were of the view that it should be copied, but the Germans were in no position to do so. Guderian pointed out that Hitler's panzer designers could never agree to such a move, not because of national pride, though that was clearly a factor, but because it was simply not possible to mass-produce the T-34. Germany was suffering a shortage of raw materials, and even at this stage of the war lacked alloys and could not turn out the T-34's aluminium diesel engines at the rate required. Essentially it was all or nothing on the Tiger and the Panther.

Guderian recalled the fateful decision: 'It was therefore decided that the following solution be adopted: the construction of the Tiger tank, a panzer of some 60 tons, which had recently been started would continue; meanwhile, a light tank, called the Panther, weighing 35 and 45 tons, was to be designed.' Hitler, though, had seriously miscalculated the importance of his panzers. In May 1940 German industries were only producing 125 panzers a month, and it was another two years before Hitler ordered production to increase to 600 a month. To make matters worse, the Tiger took twice as long to build as previous panzers. Any dreams that Hitler and his generals may have entertained about deploying large numbers of Tigers on the Eastern Front to deliver a bloody nose to the Red Army were soon dashed.

Guderian recorded, 'On 19 March 1942 [Albert] Speer [Minister for Armaments and War Production] informed the Führer that by October 1942 there would be sixty Porsche Tigers and twenty-five Henschel Tigers available, and that by March 1943 a further 135 would be produced, bringing the total by that time to 220 — assuming that they were all employable.' On the basis of these scanty figures it is hard to credit that a major war in Europe was even under way. Also, of course, the Porsche design was found wanting and would end up being converted into the Ferdinand tank destroyer.

With the Tiger I rolling off the production line, Hitler was desperate to get his new heavy tank into action as quickly as possible. Logically the crews should have been given plenty of time to practise their gunnery skills and offensive and defensive tactics, while the mechanics and technicians ironed out the inevitable design problems on the proving ground — but there was a war on. Hitler, just like the British Prime Minister Winston Churchill, was impatient to see results. Churchill had insisted that when the Crusader, Grant and Sherman tanks arrived in North Africa they be rushed to the front as quickly as possible. This had dire consequences for the ill-prepared Crusaders.

Hitler chose to ignore the warnings from his staff that his Tigers and their crews were not yet ready. Guderian lamented that the Führer would not see sense:

> A lesson learned from the First World War had taught us that it is necessary to be patient about committing new weapons and that they must be held back until they are being produced in such quantities as to allow their employment en masse. In the First World War the French and British used their tanks prematurely, in small numbers, and thereby failed to win the great victory which they were entitled to expect. ... Hitler was well aware of the facts. But he was consumed by his desire to try his new weapon.

To make matters worse, Hitler chose to dispatch the Tigers to a part of the Eastern Front that was simply not suited to their capabilities. Army Group Centre might have appreciated them on the vast open Russian steppes where their range would have given them a decided edge; instead, Hitler decided that the troublesome city of Leningrad was a greater priority. This area was covered in dense forests, lakes and swamps, none of which was ideal terrain for armoured warfare. The Tiger would not be at its best in the close confines of such a landscape. Also this geography favoured the defenders, which was partly why the Red Army had been able to cling on to Leningrad in the face of determined German attacks.

Hitler chose to deploy the Tiger I for the first time on the Leningrad front, where the wooded and swampy terrain was far from suited to tank warfare.

The German High Command should have known better. The ease with which German artillery destroyed Soviet tanks near the front lines at Leningrad once the surrounding forests had been flattened should have served as a warning. Once tanks were caught on narrow tracks and in the open, the outcome was always the same and the crews were lucky if they managed to escape. The terrain around Leningrad was simply not suited for armoured operations.

Very briefly it seemed as if Hitler had seen sense and changed his mind. His dithering over where to commit the Tigers perplexed senior German commanders, including Guderian, who grumbled,

On 8 July 1942, he [Hitler] ordered the first Tiger Companies were to be made ready with all speed for operations against Leningrad. By 23 July, that is to say fifteen days later, Hitler had changed his mind; he now demanded that the Tigers be ready for operations in France by September at the latest. It would thus appear that he was already expecting a large-scale Allied landing.

(*Above*) The appearance of the T-34 in 1941 proved a major headache for the Germans, who dubbed it 'outstanding'.

(*Opposite, top*) In contrast, the Germans easily overwhelmed the lumbering KV-1 and production was abandoned.

(*Opposite, below*) Likewise the KV-2, with its large 152mm howitzer, proved little more than a nuisance.

Hitler ignored the fact that the forests around Leningrad were not a good place to test the brand-new Tiger.

At the same time Hitler was pressing to get any technical problems resolved as quickly as possible. 'In August 1942 Hitler ordered an inquiry to be made as to how quickly the 88mm cannon could be installed in the Tiger tank,' noted Guderian. 'This gun was to be capable of firing a shell that could penetrate 200mm of armour.' He went on to add, 'Hitler insisted, quite correctly, that the Tiger be armed with the long 88mm flat trajectory gun, preferring this weapon to one of heavier calibre but lesser muzzle velocity. The primary purpose of the tank gun must be to fight enemy tanks, and to this all other considerations must be made subordinate.'

But Hitler was to change his mind again and insisted on sending a few Tigers to the Leningrad front, with predictable results. The 1st Company of Heavy Panzer Battalion 502 was the first unit to receive the brand-new Henschel Tigers. The first four were delivered on 19 and 20 August 1942. The crews were very impressed: this was a tank that you could go to war in with confidence. They marvelled at the armour and the gun.

In preparation for an anticipated Soviet attack, General Georg von Kuechler, commander of Army Group North, was ordered by the German High Command to move the 170th Infantry Division northwards from Mga, which lay south-east of Leningrad. It also sent him several Tigers that were en route from Pskov by train. Suspecting that the Soviets were driving on the Neva River via Siniavino, Kuechler ordered his 5th Mountain and 28th Jäger Divisions, earmarked for Operation Northern Light, to move from their staging areas to Mga. He also moved the 12th Panzer Division to protect the Neva and hastened the 170th Infantry's move on Siniavino.

Supported by four Panzer IIIs, the Tigers were shipped to the Leningrad front and arrived at Mga on 29 August. Kuechler committed his four Tigers to combat south of the Siniavino Heights. The crews may have been confident in their new tanks' capabilities, but they were uncomfortable trundling round the Russian forests. The rudimentary roads and tracks were not intended to take the weight of a 57-ton Tiger, and when the drivers tried to go cross-country they found the going even more unforgiving. Simply getting to the jump-off point for the attack was a struggle in itself. The transmissions quickly packed up on three of the Tigers, two of them breaking down almost immediately. By the end of the day only half were still operational and the other two had to be recovered. The Soviet penetration was contained, but the Tigers played no part in it.

Three more Tigers arrived between 16 and 18 September. The unit was sent back into action on 21 September, and this time one Tiger and three Panzer IIIs were lost. The Tiger became stuck after it bogged down, and the net result was that one of Hitler's brand-new tanks had to be destroyed. The Soviets immediately went to work trying to find ways to overcome this new Nazi war machine.

An early production Tiger I on the Eastern Front. Despite its wide tracks, the mud and ice often caused problems with the complicated overlapping road wheels.

The Tiger's restricted mobility and low speed meant it was deployed to the Eastern Front in combination with Panzer IIIs, whose task was to act as flank guards.

Guderian held Hitler personally responsible for the Tigers' failure, remarking,

He therefore ordered the Tigers to be committed in a quite secondary operation, in a limited attack carried out in terrain that was utterly unsuitable; for in the swampy forests near Leningrad heavy tanks could only move in single file along the forest tracks, which of course, was exactly where the enemy anti-tank guns were posted, waiting for them. The results were not only heavy, unnecessary, casualties, but also the loss of secrecy and of the element of surprise for future operations. Disappointment was all the greater since the attack bogged down in the unsuitable terrain.

In the meantime the rest of 1st Company, Heavy Panzer Battalion 502, did not arrive at the front until 25 November 1942, equipped with five Tigers and fourteen Panzer IIIs. Battlefield loss replacements in the shape of an additional seven Tigers were delivered in February 1943. By mid-year the company had fourteen Tigers on its strength. The battalion did not get a second company as this was reassigned to Heavy Panzer Battalion 503. Reinforcements in the shape of new 2nd and 3rd Companies did not reach the 502nd until the summer of 1943, by which time the Tiger's element of surprise had been completely lost.

The Tiger I came with two types of track, a wide one measuring 28½in for combat and a narrower one of 20½in for travel and transportation. In order to fit the narrow tracks the outer wheels were removed from each suspension unit. While the triple wheel suspension gave a smoother ride, it also meant the

interleaved wheels were susceptible to becoming fouled with mud and snow. If this clogging were allowed to freeze on the Eastern Front, it set like concrete and jammed up the wheels, leaving the Tiger completely immobilised. The Soviets soon discovered that the Tiger was vulnerable to the Russian winter and timed their attacks for the early hours, when they knew that enemy vehicles had been frozen solid during the night.

Evgeni Bessonov, who served as a lieutenant in the Red Army, later observed at first hand that mud was also a significant problem for the Tiger, when his unit was attacked by eight of them. 'The tanks were some 50 metres from us, when all of a sudden a miracle happened,' recalled Bessonov. 'The Tigers skidded on the wet soil and stopped. The tanks were stuck on one spot, their tracks spinning, but the tanks could not move. We were lucky that because of the Tiger's weight its tracks did not have good cohesion in the mud.'' Luckily for him and his men, the Tigers, lacking infantry support, withdrew.

After this very inauspicious debut, the Tigers found themselves resisting Soviet attempts to lift the siege of Leningrad when the 2nd Shock Army tried to cut its way through to Schlüsselburg on the south side of Lake Ladoga. Operation Iskra (Spark) was a Soviet offensive launched on 11 January 1943 to reopen a land corridor to the besieged city, which had been cut off since 15 September 1941 with the arrival of the German 18th Army at Schlüsselburg. After the failure of a similar offensive at the end of September 1942, the Red Army had amassed much larger forces on a smaller front to ensure they overwhelmed all before them. Overall, the Tigers were unable to make much difference to the fighting. On 12 January 1943 they knocked out twelve T-34/76 tanks. On 14 January 1943, after they managed to disable one, the Red Army got its hands on a Tiger. A second vehicle was taken a few days later.

This crewman is demonstrating for the camera just how impervious the Tiger's frontal armour was – nonetheless its initial encounters with the Red Army did not go well.

A disabled Tiger I abandoned in the snow. The Red Army captured its first Tiger in January 1943.

These two photos show the appalling conditions facing the Tiger on the Eastern Front in the spring and autumn. Seas of mud regularly swallowed up whole vehicles.

Early production Tiger Is moving up through the Russian forests ready to attack.

The Germans were so impressed with the T-34 they wanted to copy it, but instead ended up with the Tiger and Panther.

The post-mortem of what went wrong at Leningrad did not seem to dissuade Hitler from wasting his Tigers by deploying them the minute they came off the factory floor. The Tiger had good armour and stand-off capabilities (it could outshoot any tank in a face-to-face battle), so it needed to fight in open tank country where the enemy could be picked off at a distance. Deployed in sufficient numbers, it would simply overwhelm all before it. Instead, in an attempt to help Generals Rommel and von Arnim fighting in North Africa, Hitler now began to look at the hills and mountains of Tunisia.

Dismayed at the Tigers' lost opportunities, Guderian recalled,

At the beginning of December there were renewed discussions concerning the correct employment of tanks. It was then pointed out to Hitler that the commitment of the Tigers piecemeal was highly disadvantageous. He now expressed the opinion that commitment in detail was suitable for the requirements of the Eastern theatre, but that in Africa employment in mass would be more rewarding. Unfortunately I do not know on what grounds this incomprehensible statement was based.

For better or worse, Hitler was set on sending the Tigers to face the British and Americans in North Africa.

Chapter Five

Tunisian Tigers

While Hitler persuaded himself that the Henschel Tiger I was a war winner, he simply could not wait until it was fully ready for combat and available in numbers that would make its presence truly decisive. There was no escaping its poor debut on the Eastern Front, but now it was to compound this by a poor showing in North Africa. Heavy Panzer Battalion 501 was formed in Erfurt in May 1942 and intended for duty in Africa.

During the summer of that year Hitler, floundering around trying to find a use for the rejected Porsche Tigers, pressed for them to be used in North Africa. General Heinz Guderian was quick to dismiss such ideas as nonsense:

> During the discussion on the Porsche Tiger, Hitler expressed his opinion that this tank, being electrically powered and air-cooled, would be particularly suitable for employment in the African theatre, but that its operational range of only 30 miles was quite unsatisfactory and must be increased to 90 miles. This was undoubtedly correct; only it should have been stated when the first designs were submitted.

Hitler's senior commanders, including Guderian, tried to stop him dispatching the Tiger I to Tunisia in the closing months of 1942 but with no success. The situation for the surrounded German forces there was at best precarious, and few could understand the reasoning behind sending their latest and best tank to an uncertain fate. Guderian wrote in his memoirs, 'Units were still being sent over to Africa and there committed to the flames, among others our newest Tiger battalion. All argument against such a policy was quite ineffective.'

The 501st had to wait three months before it received its first Tigers. It then moved to southern France in October 1942 with twenty Tigers and sixteen Panzer IIIs. The following month the battalion travelled by rail down through Italy, and the first three Tigers of 1st Company arrived in Bizerte in Tunisia on 23 November 1942. Any illusions that the panzertruppen may have had about enjoying warmer climes in Italy, Sicily and Tunisia were soon dispelled by the winter weather. They deployed from Germany via Italy to the port of Reggio. Those involved in the move were keen

One of the Tiger Is sent to Tunisia to help Rommel, who was fighting a desperate two-front battle.

to avoid the mishaps that had beset the panzers when they had first deployed to Libya with Rommel. On that occasion a cargo ship had caught fire at Naples and sank with the loss of a dozen panzers.

Once they were off Sicily, the Tiger crews cannot have been immune to the rumours that the war was not going well across the Mediterranean, especially following the British victory at El Alamein and the American landings in French North Africa. German troops had been successfully rushed to Tunisia to protect Rommel's rear. Nonetheless the Luftwaffe flights bringing back a steady stream of wounded did little to help morale and there was unease among the Italian garrison on Sicily.

Convoys had to hug the waters off Sicily. The Mediterranean was not safe as the Allied air forces escalated their attacks on Rommel's maritime supply lines. Long-range Allied fighter-bombers and submarines operating from Malta were particular threats. Axis shipping losses in the Mediterranean were heavy, but luckily for the Germans the Tigers made the crossing unscathed.

The Tiger battalion found the docks at Bizerte and the outlying airfields bustling with activity as the Germans sought to expand and defend their bridgehead in

The rear end of an early production Tiger I captured in Tunisia by the British Army. Clearly visible are the massive exhausts and the Feifel air cleaner system on either side. The turret escape hatch on the right was installed from December 1942 onwards.

Another view of the tank, showing the remaining rear-facing pistol port on the turret.

Another Tunisian Tiger captured by the Allies.

Tunisia. This time, instead of being faced with mud and forests, the Tigers were confronted by mud, rain and mountains. The nights were also bitterly cold and the mountains were capped by snow. The Tigers first went into action in early December and throughout that month more tanks were shipped across to Africa.

The Tunisian Tigers did not get off to a good start. The first tank to arrive seized up on the dock in Bizerte; the second then broke down on the road west. Four others made for Djedeida under the eccentric Captain Nikolai Baron von Nolde, who insisted on wearing gym shoes into battle. On the morning of 2 December 1942 they smashed into the positions of the Royal Hampshire Regiment. Although the British were overrun, the Germans got a hot reception. Nolde foolishly clambered from his tank to give an order to another officer and had both his legs blown away by an anti-tank shell. A sniper killed the second exposed officer. The German attack rolled on relentlessly into Tebourba, and Allied losses included fifty-five tanks, fifty-three field guns and 300 other vehicles.

On 6 December 1942 Major Leuder, serving with the 501st, noted:

Fleeing enemy columns and tanks were observed as soon as the Tigers appeared. These fleeing enemy infantry could only be engaged with difficulty, because the hilly terrain constantly provided cover for the opponent. ...

One Tiger was hit in the idler wheel and the road wheels by a self-propelled 75mm gun. However, it remained driveable. From covered positions on the heights northwest of Medjerda, medium enemy batteries fired at the Tigers without success.

The US 1st Armored Division's 2nd Battalion had lost forty-two M3 General Grant tanks around Djedeida and Tebourba by 10 December 1942 when it was pulled out of the line. By this stage the Tiger crews had learned that they were impervious to the 75mm gun on the M3 General Grant/Lee medium tank; surprisingly, the 37mm gun on the M3 Stuart light tank was more of a nuisance. Accurate fire at the Tiger driver's visor, commander's cupola and the gap beneath the turret proved a problem. In one instance a shell fragment jammed a Tiger's turret, putting it temporarily out of action. The solution was a deflector channel similar to that on the Panzer II and III. Landmines also proved a threat to the Tiger's running gear. At 600 metres Allied 37mm and 40mm anti-tank guns were only a threat to the Tiger's road wheels and tracks. Artillery tended to cause only minor damage to the road wheels. In contrast, the Tiger's 88mm gun easily dealt with the Lee and Stuart tanks with impunity.

The panzertruppen of the 501st were not long in making field modifications to their tanks; these included altering the mudguards to cope with the dust and sand, and lowering the headlights to make them less conspicuous. The Tigers deployed to Tunisia and southern Russia were a tropical version known as the Tiger (Tp). They were fitted with a Feifel air cleaner system attached to the back of the tank and linked to the engine via the engine cover plate. This was, however, a luxury that could easily be dispensed with and it was discontinued on all production vehicles from early 1943 onwards.

The British Army claimed some success against the 501st's Tigers in early 1943, destroying one and capturing another. The British first came up against the Tiger I near Pont du Fahs, where 6-pounder anti-tank guns took on nine Panzer IIIs and two Tigers. The British had been forewarned of the attack and concealed their guns with orders to hold their fire until signalled to open up at very close range. Both the Tigers were knocked out at 300–500 yards.

The British soon found that their best weapon for countering the Tiger was the 17-pounder (76.2mm) anti-tank gun. This had similar hitting power to the German 88mm gun and had been issued to the British Army in the summer of 1942. Hurriedly mounted on a 25-pounder gun carriage, it was ordered to supplement

In Tunisia the Tiger acted in support of the much more numerous Panzer IV, seen here.

the 6-pounders in Africa. Under the codename 'Pheasant', a hundred of these prototype 17/25-pounders were rushed to North Africa and first saw action in February 1943. As a towed gun, they proved to be the best anti-tank weapon in the Allies' armoury. Installing the gun into a tank was to prove an altogether different matter.

Tigers of the 501st were involved in the attack on the US 1st Armored Division between the Faid Pass and Djebel Lessouda on 14 February 1943. On that day the 1st Armored was deployed around Djebel Lessouda, while an American observation post on the high ground was keeping watch on the Faid Pass. Reports of firing on the road from Faid began to filter in to the commander of the 1st Battalion, and the distant roar of artillery seemed to indicate some sort of firefight was going on in the direction of Lessouda. The wind coming in over the mountains threw up blinding sand which masked the advance of two battle groups from the 10th Panzer Division, numbering about sixty panzers. The Tigers spearheading the attack rumbled through the Pass with impunity. 'The Tigers are coming!' went up the cry and the lightly equipped Americans abandoned their positions in terror.

In response the 1st Armored sent forward fifteen Stuart light tanks to try to impede the attack, but, armed with just a 37mm gun, there was nothing they could do against the Tiger's 88mm gun and the 75mm gun of the Panzer IV. One after another they were destroyed, their puny rounds simply bouncing off the advancing German armour. The Shermans of the US division's inexperienced 1st Battalion were then committed to the battle, but they made little impression either and many of these tanks were soon blazing wrecks. The experiences of the US 1st Armored Division provided a stark lesson in just how foolhardy it was to pitch light tanks against German heavy and medium tanks. The net result was a major reduction in the number of light tanks deployed in American armoured divisions and their replacement by medium tanks – namely the Sherman.

Deployment of the Tigers in Tunisia soon proved to be a cause of friction between Generals Rommel and von Arnim. Rommel was irritated that these new weapons had been assigned to von Arnim's 5th Panzer Army and not placed under his command. But even if it meant lying to Rommel, von Arnim had no intention of giving up his new and powerful panzers.

For his Kasserine counterattack on 19 February 1943 Rommel wanted the Tigers to support the 10th Panzer Division's push on Thala. He later recalled,

> Before the start of the operation, we had asked von Arnim to send us the nineteen Tiger tanks which were with 5th Panzer Army. If we had these tanks at Thala, we might have been able to push on further. But von Arnim had refused our request, saying that all the tanks were under repair, a statement

When the American Stuart light tank, seen here on exercise in the US, took on the Tiger, the results were predictable and costly.

which we later discovered to have been untrue. He had wanted to hold on to the detachment of Tigers for his own offensive.

In the event 10th Panzer was forced from Thala thanks to the arrival of the British 6th Armoured Division and other units. Rommel noted on 22 February, 'I drove up to Thala again, where I was forced to the conclusion that the enemy had grown too strong for our attack to be maintained.' Rommel clearly held von Arnim responsible, adding, 'The stubborn American defence of the Kasserine Pass and the delayed arrival

Colour Plates

The following colour plates by military artist Brian Delf give a general impression of the paint schemes applied to the Tiger I and II and other variants. While the Wehrmacht issued very specific regulations and paint colours, it should be borne in mind that there were no hard and fast rules in the field (for more detailed guidance on this see 'Colour Schemes' pp. 38–42). The German vehicle base colour dunkel gelb (a deep sand yellow) has been portrayed ranging from a very pale yellow through khaki to a soft brownish sandy orange. Likewise the olivgrun (olive green) has been shown as light pea green.

Crews tended to adapt whatever paint they had to local field conditions, and the finish varied enormously depending on how the paint was applied (brush, broom, rag or spray gun) and at what thickness. Rain, dust and mud also inevitably had an impact on the paint scheme, which would fade fairly rapidly and in extreme cases even wash off. During the winter months the Tigers usually received an often very indifferent coat of whitewash that produced varying results (see pp. 20, 131, 144, 145 and 153).

Black and white photographs can help determine the shape and pattern created by the camouflage applied to the Tigers, but they give no real indication of depth of colour. Even those colour photographs of the time have probably not accurately captured the various hues and continual reproduction over the years will have distorted the colour even more. Despite the best will in the world, even museums have struggled to attain a high level of accuracy when repainting refurbished vehicles.

At the start of the war German military vehicles were painted in a two-tone scheme using dunkel grau/dark grey and dunkel braun/dark brown. While the grey provided the base coat, irregular patches of the brown were added to break up the outline of the vehicle. In mid-1940 the brown was discontinued.

In August 1944, to assist the field units, the manufacturers were ordered to apply camouflage at the factory. This was probably in recognition of the fact that painting the rough texture of the Zimmerit coating was no easy task. This created some uniformity to what became known as the 'ambush' camouflage scheme. However, when the Zimmerit was discontinued later that year, the tank factories gave the panzers only a cursory coat of dark red primer, with half the surface camouflaged. Any further embellishment was then left to the crews.

Plate I

Plates I and 2: Early Production Tiger I '111'

Although only a single model Henschel Tiger I was produced, there were a number of distinctive changes during the vehicle's production life. The initial Tiger I (seen here) is identifiable by the rubber-rimmed dish road wheels, the large Feifel air cleaners at the rear; the tall exposed commander's cupola and dual headlights. To avoid joins and welds, the Tiger I's turret was made from a single plate bent into a horseshoe shape. Initially this had a cylindrical cupola with vision slits and two machine pistol ports in the rear (clearly visible on this example).

These four views of Tiger '111' show an early production Tiger I deployed with Heavy Panzer Battalion 501/504 to Tunisia (see p. 76). It is in the basic factory colour known as dunkel gelb or deep sand yellow, though some are also believed to have been camouflaged using rotbraun or reddish brown. Dunkel gelb became the standard German military vehicle base colour from mid-February 1943. Unit turret numbers were either in black or red with white edging, while the German national identification Iron Cross tended to be painted on the hull just above the track guards. This company commander's tank featured in the pages of Hitler's propaganda magazine *Signal*, complete with camels.

Plate 2

In the case of Tunisian Tiger '131', which ended up at the Tank Museum at Bovington, despite numerous post-Second World War coats of paint there is evidence that it was originally camouflaged. Photographs of the tank's turret when it was first captured show traces of camouflage around the pistol port and on the back of the turret stowage bin. Likewise, during the tank's restoration grau grun/grey green was found on a number of the inner road wheels, while traces of gelb braun/tawny-yellow brown were discovered on the turret when the stowage bin was removed. The final camouflage pattern for the restored Tiger '131' was ultimately down to educated guesswork.

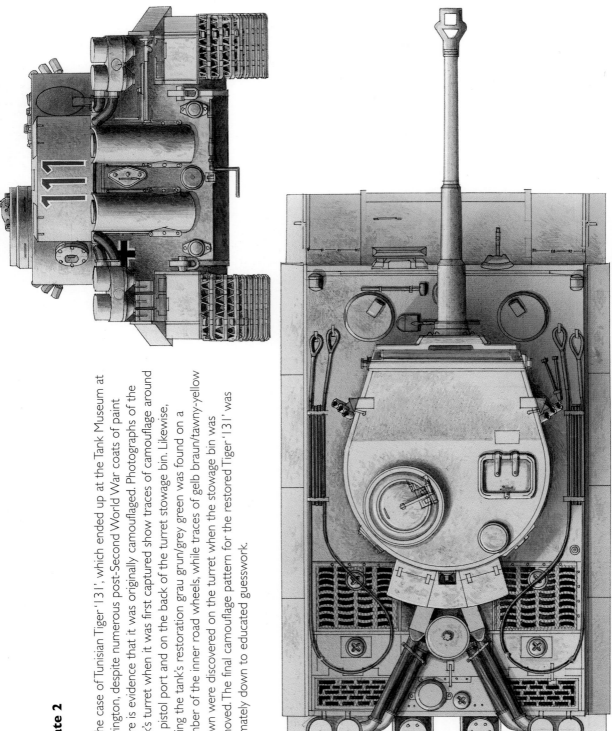

Plate 3

Plate 3: Early Production Tiger I '111' and '312'

From 1939 to 1943 German military vehicles were painted dunkel grau or panzer grey; this colour was largely intended for operations in Western Europe and had little utility in North Africa and on the Russian Steppe. Although the Germans then changed the basic vehicle colour over to dunkel gelb, during the later half of 1943 and even into 1944 they still had considerable stocks of panzer grey paint and many vehicles remained in this colour.

The early production model Tiger Is deployed with the Grossdeutschland Division and Heavy Panzer Battalions 503 and 505 at Kursk in the summer of 1943 were painted panzer grey (such as '111'), and/or deep sand yellow. The German Cross was in the centre of the hull above the track guards.

An escape hatch replaced the right-hand pistol port in December 1942; this is clearly visible on Tunisian Tiger '312'. The original cupola was replaced by a design incorporating periscopes in July 1943.

Plate 4

Plate 4: Mid-Production Tiger I '131'

This Tiger I, bearing the turret number '131', is a mid-production model in service with the Heavy SS-Panzer Battalion 101, which deployed in Normandy in the summer of 1944 (see upper image on p. 107). While the mid-production Tiger I retained the rubber-rimmed road wheels, it had a different turret that included a new, smaller, cupola. The corrugated surface on this vehicle is due to the Zimmerit anti-magnetic paste that became standard from 1943 onwards.

Photographic evidence shows that the Normandy Tigers had deep sand yellow and olive green camouflage, though it was not generally applied to the road wheels (see lower image on pp. 21 and 107); turret numbers were red with white edging, and the German Cross appeared as standard on the centre of the hull above the track guards.

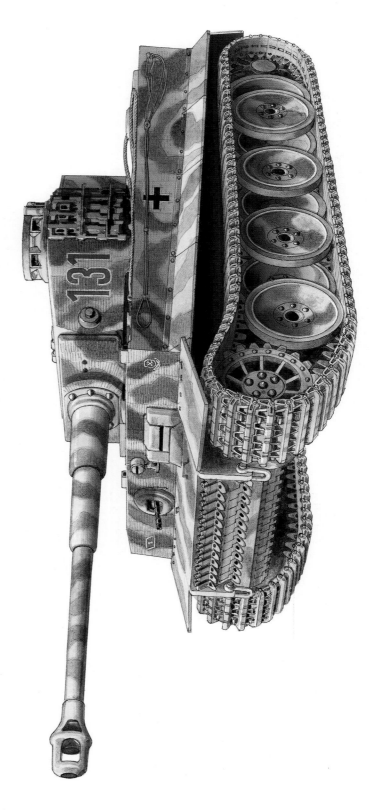

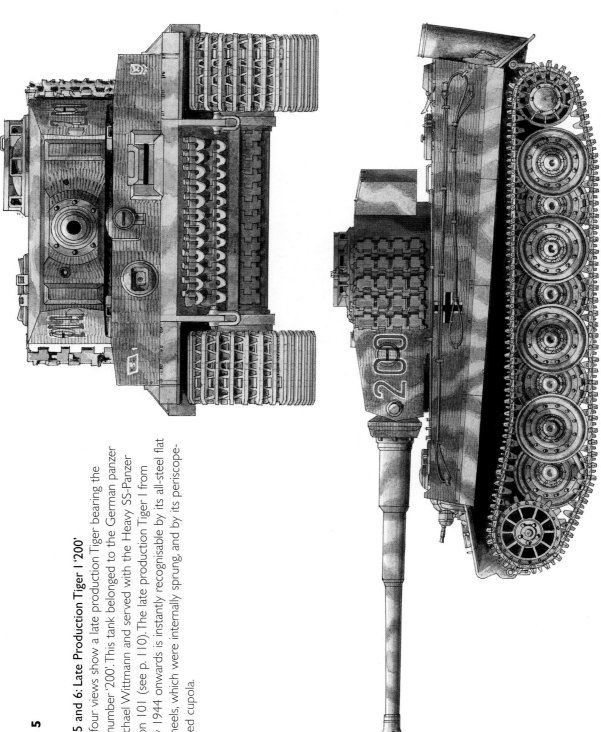

Plate 5

Plates 5 and 6: Late Production Tiger I '200'

These four views show a late production Tiger bearing the turret number '200'. This tank belonged to the German panzer ace Michael Wittmann and served with the Heavy SS-Panzer Battalion 101 (see p. 110). The late production Tiger I from January 1944 onwards is instantly recognisable by its all-steel flat disc wheels, which were internally sprung, and by its periscope-equipped cupola.

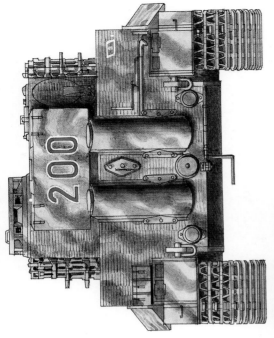

Plate 6

Plate 7a

Plate 7a and b: Late Production Tiger I '313' and '300'

Tiger I '313' is a late production model in service with the Heavy Panzer Battalion 503, again in Normandy in the summer of 1944. It was painted deep sand yellow with some olive green and reddish brown camouflage, but not the wheels; the turret numbers again appeared in red or black with white edging, with the German Cross on the centre of the hull above the track guards.

Tiger I '300' is also a late production model, which served with the Heavy Panzer Battalion 505 on the Eastern Front in the summer of 1944. It is finished with deep sand yellow plus some reddish brown camouflage; note the vehicle number appears on the gun mantlet, in black with white edging, but there is no German Cross. Carrying spare track links on the turret helped enhance the armour but tended to obscure the vehicle identification number, so alternative locations were sometimes used.

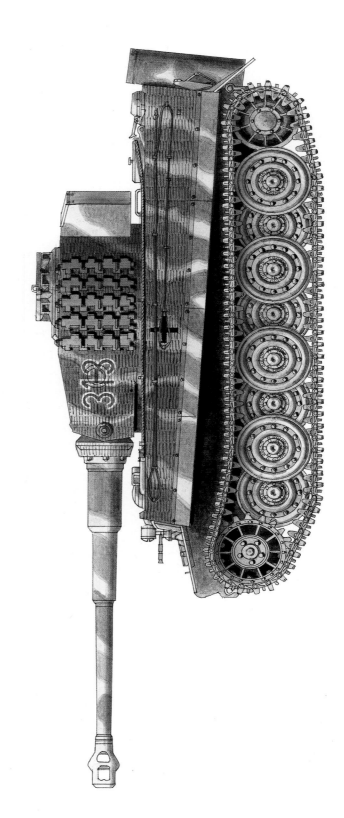

Plate 7b

Plate 8

Plate 8: Ferdinand Jagdpanzer

Ferdinand '50', from Heavy Panzerjäger Battalions 653/654, fought at Kursk during the summer of 1943. Note the lack of a hull machine gun. This vehicle utilised the rejected Porsche-designed Tiger I chassis; it has a deep sand yellow and reddish brown camouflage, with the superstructure number in white with no edging, and the German Cross on the centre of the hull above the track guards. Ferdinand '50' was extensively photographed by the Red Army (see pp. 50 and 97), and although the Ferdinand did not fare very well at Kursk, the camouflage scheme was quite effective on the open steppe.

Plate 9

Plate 9: Sturmtiger

This Sturmtiger, utilising the late production Tiger I's all-steel disc wheeled chassis, was deployed to the Eastern Front in August 1944 sporting a deep sand yellow, olive green and reddish brown camouflage. It was originally intended to support the street fighting in the Soviet Union but by the time it came into service its rationale had long passed (see p. 44), except for limited service during the Warsaw Uprising. Its small numbers and slow rate of fire ensured that it saw very little combat.

One Sturmtiger that was captured intact by US troops and photographed on 14 April 1945 has a clear two- or three-tone camouflage pattern covered in an alternating dark/light stipple effect; this appears to be a version of the later 'ambush' scheme similar to that used during the Ardennes offensive. The example at the German Panzermuseum in Munster is simply a sandy colour.

Plate 10

Plates 10 and 11: Tiger II '300'

This Tiger II '300' with the Henschel turret belonged to a unit that deployed to France in 1944. Its colour scheme consisted of the regular deep sand yellow with olive green and reddish brown camouflage, with the turret number in red or black with white edging, and the German Cross just to the right of the number.

Similar colours and schemes have been applied to the Tank Museum's Tiger II '300' with the Krupp/Porsche turret (which was captured at the Sennelager training grounds in Germany in 1945) and to Tiger II '104' with the redesigned Henschel turret (which was captured in Normandy in 1944). This camouflage scheme remained fairly standard until the winter of 1944/45, when the Tiger IIs adopted a very distinctive dotted/stipple effect ambush scheme.

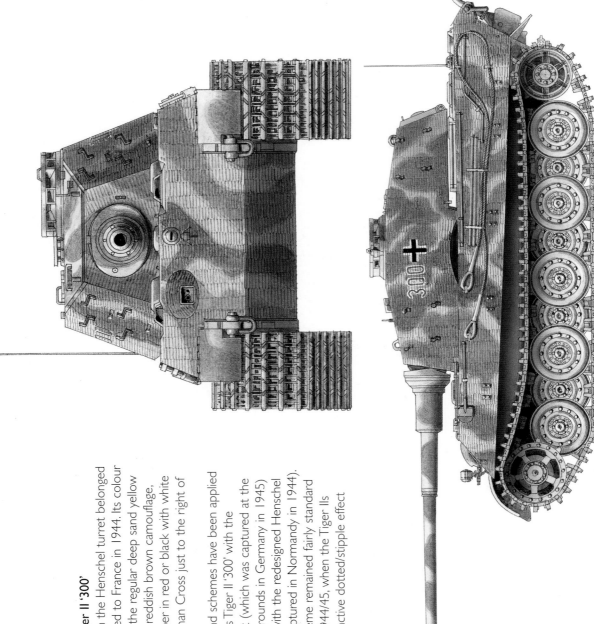

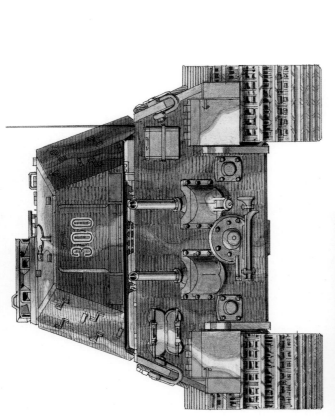

Plate 11

Plate 12

Plate 12: Tiger II '114' and '233'

Tiger II '114', with the distinctive 'Porsche' turret, serving with the Heavy Panzer Battalion 503 in Normandy during the summer of 1944 (see pp. 32, 34, 36 and 122). It has the standard deep sand yellow with olive green and reddish brown camouflage; the turret number is red with white edging, with the German Cross behind the turret number.

Tiger II '233' has a Henschel turret with the flat mantlet that did away with the dangerous rounded shot trap under the barrel.

This vehicle was deployed with Heavy Panzer Battalion 503 during Operation Panzerfaust, conducted in Budapest in October 1944. Once again the colours are deep yellow sand with olive green and reddish brown camouflage, with the German Cross behind the number (see pp. 126–7). This paint scheme would have been of little value on the streets of Budapest.

Plate 13

Plate 13: Tiger II '204'

Tiger II '204', with the Henschel turret, serving with Heavy SS-Panzer Battalion 501 during the Ardennes offensive in December 1944. It is painted bright sand yellow with olive green and reddish brown camouflage, with the Ardennes ambush scheme dotted/stipple effect. It is notable from the photographic evidence that those Tiger IIs committed to the Ardennes battle did not have the Zimmerit coating, hence the smooth hull and turret of this example (and see pp. 31, 37 and 40–1). Intended as a breakthrough panzer, the Tiger II ended up fighting futile defensive actions that ironically capitalised on this ambush paint scheme.

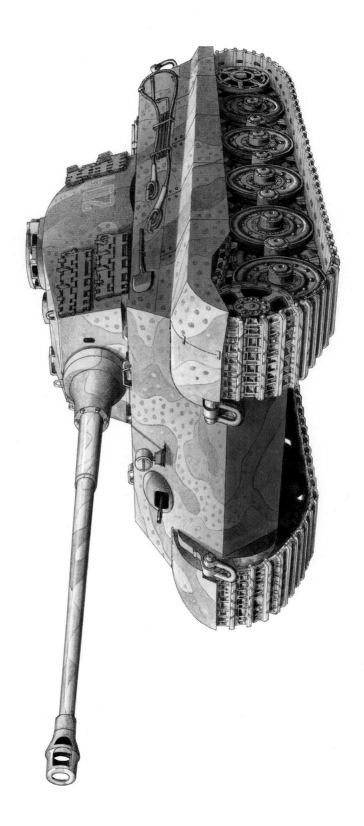

Plate 14

Plate 14: Jagdtiger

This Jagdtiger is finished in the regulation camouflage of deep sand yellow, olive green and red brown – see also the rather indistinct schemes on p. 153 (upper image) and p. 155 (lower image) – but most of those captured in 1945 simply had their factory finish, as in the closing months of the war the crews did not have the opportunity or indeed the desire to paint them (see pp. 54, 55 and 146–7).

The Tank Museum's Jagdtiger was a training vehicle captured at Sennelager, Germany. It was the second one fitted with the Porsche suspension using the longitudinal torsion bars rather than the more common transverse type. Although it was a training vehicle, parts of the hull on the front and sides were coated in haphazard patches of Zimmerit. This example is painted panzer grey with olive green blotches. In contrast Jagdtiger '331', which was shipped to America, had a pale grey and brown camouflage scheme and no Zimmerit coating (see p. 153, upper image).

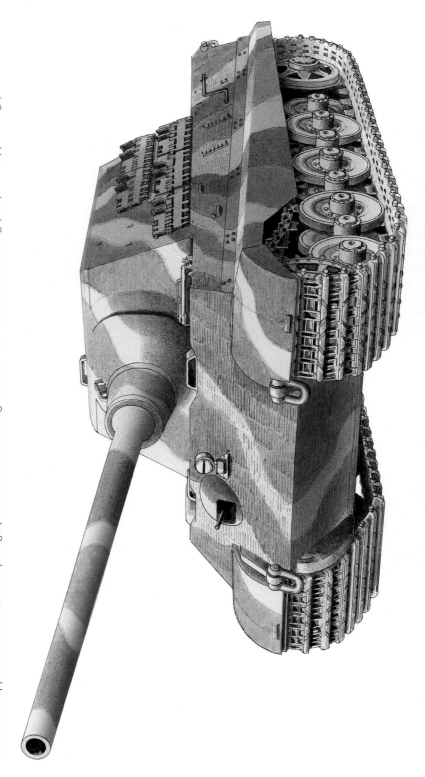

of the 5th Army's forces prevented us from making a surprise break into the enemy hinterland.'

Tired and weary, Rommel argued that if von Arnim had sent him the Tigers and more infantry, he might well have succeeded. 'That may be true,' responded Field Marshal Kesselring, 'but you had the authority to overrule von Arnim. Why didn't you?'

Four days later the 5th Panzer Army, employing the Tigers, opened its own attack at Medjez el Bab, 40 miles west of Tunis. The initial breakthrough was soon met with heavy counterattacks. Rommel was furious:

> It made me particularly angry to see how the few Tigers we had in Africa, which had been denied us for our offensive in the south, were thrown into attack through a marshy valley, where their principal advantage – the long range of their heavy guns – was completely ineffective. The heavy tanks either stuck fast in the mud, or were pounded into immobility by the enemy. Of the nineteen Tigers which went into action, fifteen were lost.

While the German High Command was filled with optimism following the mauling of the American Army at Kasserine, Rommel knew that the presence of a few Tigers was not ultimately going to affect the final outcome of the battle for North Africa. Commenting on the Americans' resources, he observed, 'their armament in anti-tank weapons and armoured vehicles was so enormous that we could look forward with but small hope of success to the coming mobile battles'. Rommel was also dismayed at the weight of American air power, which came into play once the bad weather that had masked his attack lifted.

By the end of February Heavy Panzer Battalion 501 could muster eighteen Tigers but on 1 March seven were destroyed by their crews, then on 17 March the survivors were attached to Heavy Tank Battalion 504. This was the second Tiger unit to be dispatched to North Africa. It was formed from two companies of men from Panzer Regiment 4 in mid-January 1943 at Fallingbostel. The battalion was issued with two Command Tigers, eighteen Tiger Is and twenty-five Panzer IIIs.

They arrived in Italy in early March and the first three Tigers serving with the 1st Company reached Tunisia on 12 March. Shortly afterwards eleven Tigers of Heavy Panzer Battalion 501 joined them. The 2nd Company remained on Sicily. During late March and early April Tigers continued to be delivered to Bizerte with the last one arriving on 16 April 1943. During a three-day period four Tigers were lost in action, including the one preserved at Bovington Tank Museum.

Hitler soon lost interest in the fate of his Tiger tanks and, indeed, the rest of the Afrika Korps. As Inspector General of the Panzertruppen, Guderian was reporting by mid-April 1943,

The American M3 Grant medium tank also received a mauling at the hands of the Tiger in Tunisia.

The situation in Africa had become hopeless, and I asked [General] Schmundt to help me arrange that the many superfluous tank crews – particularly the irreplaceable commanders and technicians with years of experience behind them – be now flown out. Either I failed to convince Schmundt or else he did not press my arguments with sufficient energy to Hitler, for when I next saw the Führer and personally mentioned the matter I met with no success. The question of prestige – as so often – proved more powerful than common sense.

The Americans found their treatment by the Tigers in Tunisia very sobering. One American colonel, reporting on its qualities in 1943, noted: 'I have inspected the battlefield at Faid Pass in Tunisia, being with the force which retook it. Inspection of our tanks destroyed there indicated that the 88mm gun penetrated into the turret from the front and out again in the rear. Few gouges were found indicating that all strikes had made penetrations.'

Yank, the US Army Weekly, could not help striking a triumphal note when it featured a knocked-out Tiger on its cover, captioned 'This vicious-looking machine, photographed by *Yank*'s Sgt George Aarons during the Tunisian campaign, is a PzKW VI (Panzer Kampfwagen), which translates literally as armored battlewagon. More often it was called the Tiger, but here with the sleeve knocked off its 88mm cannon and resting against the muzzle brake, it is definitely a tamed one.'

Tiger crews soon found that their armour was impervious to the M3's hull-mounted 75mm anti-tank gun.

Understandably both the British and US armies were keen to evaluate the 'tamed' Tigers captured in Tunisia as quickly as possible. The US Army shipped a captured Tiger tank back to the Aberdeen Ordnance Research Center's proving grounds in America and *Yank* reported in late January 1944:

> Specially assigned recovery crews, ordnance men trained to know and work with enemy material, roam the battlefields of the world to collect the captured rolling stock, which is being accumulated here. It arrives with the dust of its respective theater still on it, plus the names and addresses of GIs who scratch *Bizerte* or *Attu* or *Buna* mission in big letters on the paint.
>
> The famous Tiger, the largest and heaviest German tank. Weighing 61½ tons, it is propelled at a speed of from 15 to 18 miles an hour by a 600-to-650 horsepower Maybach V-12 cylinder engine. Maybach engines are used in many of the Nazi panzerwagonen and in submarines. The PzKW VI has an armor thickness which ranges from 3¼ to 4 inches. An additional slab of steel mounted in conjunction with its 88-mm forms frontal armor for the turret. Besides the long-barreled 88, it carries two MG34 (Model 1934) machine guns. The largest tank used in combat by any nation today, the Tiger is more than 20 feet long, about 11¾ feet wide and 9¾ feet high. It has a crew of five.
>
> The engineers, who judge by the mass of detail employed in all German-built machines, are convinced that the Nazi idea has been to sacrifice speed for overall performance and manoeuvrability. The German equipment, from the sleek motorcycle to the massive PzKW VI, is rugged.

Along with the rest of the German and Italian armies, both Tiger units surrendered in Tunisia on 12 May 1943. Afterwards Guderian argued there was no point in leaving them on Sicily in the face of an impending Allied invasion. Recalling how the Tigers had been needlessly wasted in North Africa, he recorded with some bitterness,

> the same thing was to happen in the defence of Sicily. On this occasion, when I urged that the Tigers be withdrawn to the mainland, Goering [commander of the Luftwaffe] joined in the argument with the remark: 'But Tigers can't pole-vault across the Straits of Messina. You must realise that, Colonel-General Guderian!' I replied: 'If you have really won air supremacy over the Straits of Messina, the Tigers can come back from Sicily the same way they went out.' The air expert fell silent; the Tigers remained in Sicily.

Predictably the remaining seventeen Tigers serving with the 2nd Company, Heavy Panzer Battalion 504, were lost on Sicily following the American and British landings on the island. The survivors were then regrouped in Italy and continued to fight there until the end of the war, equipped with Tiger Is.

The remains of smashed Tiger tanks on the road to Tunis.

Probably the most famous Tiger I in the world came from Tunisia. It belongs to the British Tank Museum at Bovington and is the only example restored to full working order. Tiger 131 was selected to be sent back to Britain and immediately acquired a celebrity status in light of the VIPs who came to see it. The tank had been knocked out during an engagement at Medjez-el-Bab on 21 April 1943 with British Churchill tanks of 4 Troop, A Squadron, 48th Royal Tank Regiment.

Royal Electrical & Mechanical Engineers recovered the Tiger using a bulldozer and it arrived in Tunis on 24 May 1943. The following month it was examined by King George VI, Winston Churchill and Anthony Eden. Afterwards it was moved to La Goulette and from there to Bizerte by landing craft. It was subsequently shipped to

The final resting place of another Tiger in Tunisia. Too few were committed to the battle to stave off German defeat.

Glasgow, where it arrived on 8 October 1943, and was sent to the Department of Tank Design in Surrey. It was displayed as a war trophy on Horse Guards Parade in London, and Londoners were able to gawp at Hitler's latest panzer until the end of 1943, when it was dismantled for technical assessment. Subsequently, in 1951, Tiger 131 was given to the Tank Museum at Bovington, where it has been ever since.

In the meantime, thanks to Hitler's haste, not only had the Russians got hold of the Tiger, but so too had the Americans and British – before it had even been deployed in any significant numbers. This was to have serious ramifications for its subsequent performance in Russia and Normandy.

Chapter Six

Tiger I on the Steppes

Despite its disappointing showing at Leningrad and in Tunisia, Guderian remained determined to get the most out of the Tiger. In late March 1943 he visited General von Mellenthin's 48th Panzer Corps. 'Guderian particularly wanted to discuss the experiences of the Tiger battalion of the Grossdeutschland Division in the recent offensive,' von Mellenthin later recalled, 'and Count Strachwitz, the very dashing commander of their panzer regiment, was able to give him many interesting details regarding the performance and limitations of the new tank. As a result of his visit Guderian ordered a speed-up in the production of Tigers and Panthers.'

Grossdeutschland received the Tiger before many other units, forming a heavy panzer battalion from the summer of 1943. In fact, as early as January 1943 the Grossdeutschland Panzer Regiment had formed a heavy tank company that comprised nine Tiger Is and ten Panzer IIIs. These shipped to the Eastern Front the following month, arriving at Poltava in time for the offensive to retake Kharkov. By the time of the Kursk offensive, the unit had been officially dubbed the 9th Company and was equipped with about a dozen Tigers.

In addition, Heavy Panzer Battalion 505 was created in early 1943 and by May had twenty Tigers and twenty-five Panzer IIIs. At the end of April it was assigned to Army Group Centre and shipped to the Eastern Front. From 8 to 10 June it received eleven more Tigers. Therefore at the start of Operation Citadel the battalion had thirty-one Tigers, plus supporting Panzer IIIs, and four days into the fighting, on 9 July, it was joined by the 3rd Company.

At the time of the Kursk offensive Army Group South had a total of 102 Tigers deployed with the 2nd, 3rd and 48th Panzer Corps. Heavy Panzer Battalion 503 had been earmarked to join Rommel in North Africa but instead found itself in southern Russia during the Don campaign and the retreat from Stalingrad. It had anticipated receiving the Porsche-designed Tiger, but with the cancellation of this programme the unit was equipped with twenty Henschel Tigers and twenty-five Panzer IIIs in late 1942. By April of the following year it had forty-five Tigers on its strength. The battalion was able to muster forty-two operational Tigers in time for the Kursk offensive, but these were divided up between three panzer divisions.

(*Above*) A 1st SS Panzer Division Tiger on the Eastern Front. This is a mid-production model: although it has the rubber-rimmed wheels, the turret is fitted with a cupola featuring periscopes and a side-swinging hatch which is open.

(*Opposite, top*) Officers of the Imperial Japanese Army inspect an early model Tiger in Russia.

(*Opposite, below*) The open killing grounds of the Russian steppe on which the Tiger so excelled.

Other panzer units serving with Army Group South were also equipped with Tigers; these included the 9th Company, Panzer Regiment Grossdeutschland, part of Grossdeutschland Panzergrenadier Division, which had twelve operational Tigers at the start of Kursk; and the 13th Company, 1st SS Panzer Regiment, the 8th Company, 2nd SS Panzer Regiment, and the 9th Company, 3rd SS Panzer Regiment, which had twelve each, serving with the 1st, 2nd and 3rd SS Panzer Divisions respectively.

By 1943 the German High Command knew that, despite what was said publicly, it was simply not in a position to win on the Eastern Front. At best, it could bleed the resources of the Red Army to such an extent that Stalin would be forced to the negotiating table. Hitler's generals, though, were hoping that the newly deployed quality tanks would help them counter the Red Army's superior numbers. Indeed, for the first time since Barbarossa, the German Army was fielding tanks and self-propelled guns that had a distinctive qualitative edge. Guderian recalled that the army was pinning great hopes on Hitler's new panzers: 'the Chief of the General Staff [General Zeitzler] believed that by employing the new Tigers and Panthers, from which he expected decisive successes, he could regain the initiative'.

For his summer Kursk offensive, dubbed Operation Zitadelle (Citadel), Hitler was placing great faith in his 'zoo' of tanks and fighting vehicles named after wild beasts, notably the Tiger, Panther, Elefant, Rhinoceros, Bison and Grizzly Bear. It was hoped that these would tear great holes in the ranks of the Soviet tank corps, with the Tigers, Panthers and Ferdinands able to stand off and destroy Soviet armour at great distance. If they could keep the Soviet tank numbers at arm's length and stop them closing, this would prevent the panzers from being overwhelmed.

Most if not all of the Tiger's teething problems had been ironed out after its debut at Leningrad the previous summer. The Tiger's 88mm KwK 36 anti-tank gun could rip open 100mm of armour at over 1,000 yards (1,000m) and could easily defeat the T-34 Model 1943. The T-34 had a maximum of 70mm frontal armour and even at 1,000 yards was already vulnerable to the Panzer IV Ausf F2's 75mm Kwk 40 L/43, which could penetrate 87mm of armour; it was likewise unable to counter the subsequent Panzer IV Ausf G and H, both armed with the Kwk40 L/48.

By contrast, the new Panther was undeniably a rushed job, and sorting out on-going technical problems in the heat of the battle was hardly a recipe for success. Nonetheless, its 75mm Kwk 42 L/70 anti-tank gun was a formidable weapon and could pierce 90mm of armour at 500 yards (457m) or 80mm at 1,000 yards (915m). This meant that it was capable of killing a T-34 at 875 yards (800m), while from the side it could manage this at three times the range. Well-trained and experienced crews were capable of knocking out tanks at even greater ranges. This stand-off capability meant it was fatal for Soviet tanks to engage the Tiger and the Panther in the open.

The T-34's 76.2mm gun could penetrate the Panther's side armour from 1,100 yards (1,000m), but could only penetrate the glacis armour at 330 yards (300m) and could not overcome the turret frontal armour at all. An improved armoured-piercing round was not introduced until October 1943. Although the Panther's frontal armour was on a par with the Tiger's, its side armour was little better than that of the Panzer IV.

The cumbersome Ferdinand self-propelled gun, constructed on the chassis of the failed Porsche design for the Tiger I, armed with an 88mm PaK 43 (L/71), was able to penetrate Soviet tanks at extreme range. Unfortunately in their haste to build the Ferdinand, the designers saw fit not to include any machine guns, and this had inevitable consequences on the battlefield. While the Ferdinand's 200mm of armour meant it was impervious to most Soviet guns, its 65-tonne weight meant it could only manage a grindingly slow 10km/h off-road. The thought of being under intense enemy fire while travelling at such slow speeds cannot have been very encouraging for the crew.

While the Tiger had an undeniable air of menace and the Panther a certain deadly grace, thanks to its sloping armour, the crews must have looked at the Ferdinand with a sense of despair. It was little more than a lumbering mobile pillbox, which, while packing a powerful anti-tank gun, had very limited traverse. Anyone could see that it was an ill-conceived venture; like the newly commissioned Nashhorn, it was essentially a defensive weapon that was not suited to offensive warfare.

Crucially, none of these new armoured vehicles was available in decisive numbers. Notably, there were just a hundred Tigers, about two hundred Panthers and ninety Ferdinands; over a thousand older Panzer IIIs and IVs formed the backbone of the panzer forces. The Tigers and all the other panzers had their work cut out.

During a conference in May 1943 Guderian had noted that General Model had good intelligence,

> which showed that the Russians were preparing deep and very strong defensive positions in exactly those areas where the attack by the two army groups was to go in. The Russians had already withdrawn the mass of their mobile formations from the forward area of their salient; in anticipation of a pincer attack, as proposed in this plan of ours, they had strengthened the localities of our possible break-throughs with unusually strong artillery and anti-tank forces.

General von Mellenthin, commanding 48th Panzer Corps, which included the Grossdeutschland Tigers, recalled, 'The ground rose slightly to the north, thus favouring

(*Above*) A side view of the Ferdinand's bulky silhouette. This Tiger-based tank-destroyer made its debut at Kursk.

(*Opposite, top*) Another Ferdinand moving up to the front. Without adequate panzer and infantry support, Ferdinands proved very vulnerable at Kursk.

(*Opposite, below*) The Tiger and Ferdinand made short work of the T-34, but were unable to overcome the Red Army's superior numbers and defences.

the defender. Roads consisted of tracks through the sand and became impassable for all motor transport during rain. Large cornfields covered the landscape and made visibility difficult. All in all it was not "good tank country", but it was by no means "tank proof".

The Soviet defences in the Kursk salient were formidable. By June 1943 some 300,000 civilians had been marshalled to dig a series of eight in-depth defences stretching back almost 110 miles. Using brute strength, picks and shovels, they had carved almost 3,100 miles of trenches across the landscape. Minefields sealed off the trenches and fire support positions.

The fields of wheat and corn ripening in the summer sun concealed a deadly threat. In the killing grounds between the strongpoints the sappers meticulously concealed about 2,400 anti-tank mines and a further 2,700 anti-personnel mines per mile. Initially, as the panzers and supporting infantry struggled through the minefields, they would be deluged by artillery and mortar fire. Once through this, the Tigers would encounter Soviet anti-tank defences or 'pakfronts', consisting of emplaced 76.2mm anti-tank guns supported by anti-tank rifles, machine guns and mortars. The plan was that along the expected axes of attack the German armour would meet clusters of anti-tank guns, whose job it was to funnel the panzers into yet more minefields.

Zitadelle was doomed from the start. It got under way on 4 July 1943, making little headway before being checked by the Soviet defences. The Tigers charged forwards, though many troop commanders must have been torn between standing off and destroying as many Soviet tanks as possible, and closing to escape the anti-tank mines, anti-tank guns and heavy artillery (especially the heavy howitzers) that were quickly turning the Kursk steppe into a panzer graveyard.

The need to clear the Soviet minefields and the front echelon weapons positions meant that only the 20th Panzer Division was involved in the initial assault. They achieved some success, pushing through the Soviet 15th Rifle Division's front-line trenches at 0900 and fighting their way between Bobrik and Gnilets. Barging the Soviet 321st Rifle Regiment out of the way, they secured Bobrik, 3 miles behind the Soviet lines.

On their left the 6th Infantry Division thrust down the Oka Valley, supported by Tigers of Heavy Panzer Battalion 505. The Soviet T-34s and anti-tank guns were unable to stop them taking the village of Butyrki. This exposed the Soviet 81st Rifle Division, which was busy trying to fend off the 292nd Infantry Division. The heavy Ferdinands initially ploughed through the Soviet lines with impunity, reaching Alexsandrovka, but they soon found they could not deal with the swarms of Soviet infantry. The German 86th Infantry Division reached Ponyri late that afternoon, while the 78th and 216th Infantry Divisions fought their way through the Soviet

Following their experiences at Leningrad, to counter the Tiger the Soviets came up with the SU-152 but only a few were available for Kursk.

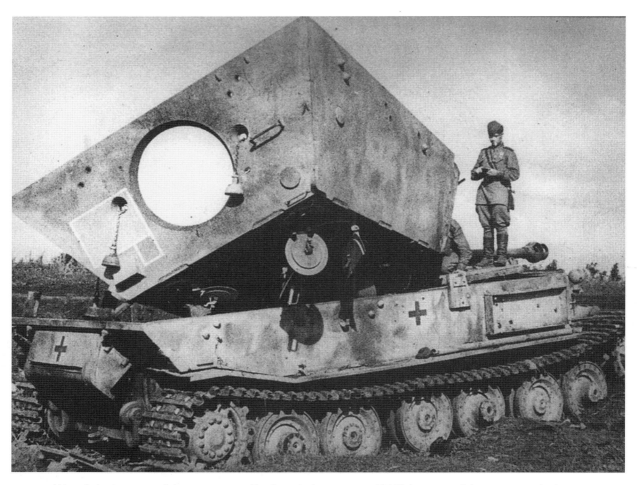

(*Above*) A close-up of the torn-apart Ferdinand shown on p. 57. If the crew did not escape before the massive blast, they would have been killed instantly.

(*Opposite, top*) Another captured Ferdinand, its armour peppered with dents, testifying to the amount of punishment it took before succumbing.

(*Opposite, below*) This Ferdinand seems to have fallen prey to mines that have severed the track and damaged the road wheels. (It may be the same vehicle as that shown on pp. 50 and 141.

defences toward the road junction at Malaorkhangelsk with the support of Ferdinands.

Individually the Tigers worked wonders. On 6 July Tigers led the charge of the 1st and 2nd SS Panzer Divisions up the Belgorod–Oboyan road. The Soviet 51st Rifle Division was pushed out of the way as the Tigers came face to face with the T-34 tanks of the 5th Guards Tank Corps south of Iakovlevo.

One German witness recalled:

> On separate slopes, some 1,000m [1,100 yards] apart, the forces face one another like figures on a chessboard, trying to influence fate, move by move, in their own favour. All the Tigers fired. The combat escalated into an ecstasy of roaring engines. The humans who directed and serviced them had to be calm; very calm, they aimed rapidly, they loaded rapidly, they gave orders quickly. They rolled ahead a few metres, pulled right, manoeuvred to escape the enemy crosshairs and bring the enemy into their own fire. We counted the torches of the enemy dead which would never again fire on German soldiers. After one hour twelve T-34s were in flames. The other thirty curved wildly back and forth, firing as rapidly as their barrels would deliver. They aimed well but our armour was very strong.

One of the most fiercely contested points in the Kursk salient was the village of Ponyri. Trying to ease the pressure, the Germans launched the Tigers of Heavy Panzer Battalion 505 and the 2nd and 20th Panzer Divisions between Samodurovka and Ollkhovatka. However, those forces that broke through were surrounded by a Soviet counterattack. After an attack at Ponyri and at the 1st May State Farm by a Soviet rifle division on 8 July, the Soviets claimed to have knocked out sixteen Tigers and twenty-four medium tanks.

Several German tank aces starred in the Kursk offensive. Most notably, Sergeant Franz Staudegger was getting his Tiger repaired at Teterevino on 8 July when a report came in that up to sixty Soviet tanks were heading his way. Hurriedly fixing their panzer, he and his crew spent two hours knocking out seventeen enemy tanks. When the Soviets finally withdrew, Staudegger gave chase and caught them hiding in a gully, where he knocked out another five T-34s. Two days later he became the first Waffen-SS Tiger commander to gain the Knight's Cross.

Similarly Second Lieutenant Michael Wittmann, who was commanding a troop of Tigers with the 1st SS Panzer Division, also achieved great success. On the first day of Operation Citadel he claimed eight enemy tanks destroyed. It was his troop that broke the attack of the Soviet 181st Tank Brigade at Prokhorovka on 12 July. During the fighting around Kursk he and his crew claimed thirty enemy tanks and twenty-eight anti-tank guns destroyed.

The T-34 could not win a stand-off fight with either the Tiger or the Ferdinand, and had to close as quickly as possible or suffer this fate.

A late production Tiger with the all-steel wheels that were introduced in January 1944.

(*Above*) An early production Tiger serving with the 2nd SS Panzer Division.

(*Opposite, top*) The fate of many Tigers once the enemy got behind them.

(*Opposite, below*) An early Tiger somewhere on the Eastern Front. All panzertruppen disliked fighting in or near woods where they were vulnerable at close range. (This tank is also shown on p. 27.)

Heavy Panzer Battalion 505 lost three Tigers on 7 July and three days later had twenty-six Tigers and five Panzer IIIs operational. On the 17th another two Tigers were lost in action, with a third lost three days later. In total, the battalion lost four Tigers during Kursk itself and another six by the end of July. During August twelve Tigers were lost. Afterwards the unit moved to the Smolensk area and was subsequently issued with new production Tigers that featured steel-rimmed wheels, cast cupolas and Zimmerit anti-magnetic mine coating. It later fought with the 24th and 25th Panzer Divisions in East Prussia. Heavy Panzer Battalion 503 lost four Tigers during the Kursk offensive and another four during its withdrawal. It received twelve replacements during August 1943.

While the Tiger proved a great success at Kursk, inflicting staggering losses on the Soviet tanks, there were simply too few of them. The 1st SS Panzer Regiment destroyed ninety tanks in the space of three hours on one day alone but still the enemy kept coming. While the crews now knew how to get the most out of the Tiger, this did not make up for their limited numbers. Once the Soviet tankers had closed in on them, the Tigers' advantage of range and thick armour was lost.

The Soviets did all they could to counter the Tiger. As General von Mellenthin recalled, they 'produced an improved model of the T-34, and finally in 1944 the massive Stalin tank which gave our Tigers plenty of trouble. The Russian tank designers understand their job thoroughly; they cut out refinements and concentrated on essentials – gun power, armour and cross-country performance.'

In response to the Tiger, the Red Army produced the SU-152. Based on a redesigned KV-1 chassis, it was armed with a massive 152mm howitzer that could be used in an anti-tank role. Fortunately for the Germans, only twelve were available for Kursk, though they accounted for twelve Tigers and seven Ferdinands, and as a result the SU-152 gained a reputation as a 'Beast-killer'. The mighty ISU-152 appeared in late 1943 as a successor to the SU-152, and also gained the nickname 'Animal-' or 'Beast- killer'. Also armed with a powerful 152mm howitzer, the ISU-152s were grouped into independent heavy assault gun regiments and brigades, which were attached to the tank corps in a support role. By the time of Operation Bagration in the summer of 1944, the Red Army had 295 ISU-152s and ISU-122s.

Chapter Seven

Tiger I in the Hedgerows

After its less than decisive showing in Tunisia and Russia, the Tiger was to gain a far greater reputation in Normandy in northern France.

At 0800 hours on 13 June 1944 a mixed British tank and infantry force led by the 4th County of London Yeomanry (the 'Sharpshooters') Armoured Regiment, and A Company, 1st Battalion, Rifle Brigade, occupied Villers-Bocage almost unopposed. The series of brutal engagements fought that day involving the Tiger rendered it impossible for the British to hold the town. Their forces were split in two, with one group trapped at Villers-Bocage and the other at Tracy-Bocage several miles to the west; the 7th Armoured Division was left exposed along the road to Livry.

The 7th Armoured's initial intelligence estimated that up to forty Tigers from 2nd Panzer and other units were in the area, with which it was feared the Germans would cut the road between Villers-Bocage and Caumont, trapping B Squadron. This estimate was not accurate: 2nd Panzer had no Tigers and its panzers did not begin to arrive from Paris until 18 June; likewise the 12th SS Panzer Division had no Tigers, and it is doubtful whether Heavy SS-Panzer Battalion 101 had more than a handful in the Villers-Bocage area on 13 June.

Sited at the head of the Seulles valley, Villers-Bocage dominated the approaches to Mont Pincon 10 miles to the south, the Odon valley and Caen in the east. The road network for the whole region stemmed from the village, making it of strategic importance to both sides: control of Villers-Bocage meant control of the roads. Regrettably, the late arrival of 7th Armoured Division's second armoured brigade from Britain due to bad weather meant the division lacked 150 tanks and supporting infantry.

What the British did not know was that the 2nd Panzer Division had been alerted to move from Amiens to Normandy to establish blocking positions in this sector, and that elements of Heavy SS-Panzer Battalion 101, from the 1st SS Panzer Corps Reserve, including Lieutenant Michael Wittmann, had occupied Point 213. The British were outclassed from the start. The Cromwell tank, which had replaced 7th Armoured Division's Shermans when they left Italy, was too lightly armoured and

(*Above*) Getting the Tigers to Normandy in the face of Allied air attacks proved a real problem – hence all the foliage.

(*Opposite, top*) Tigers of Heavy SS-Panzer Battalion 101 photographed east of Rouen on 10 June 1944.

(*Opposite, below*) The battalion at Morgny. This is clearly a mid-production Tiger.

armed. In stark contrast, the Tiger tank could expect to remain unharmed by the majority of Allied tanks except at point-blank range.

Wittmann had already established himself as a tank ace. By December 1942 he had become a second lieutenant and the following year was given command of a Tiger I in 13th Company, Leibstandarte SS-Panzer Regiment. When he was promoted to full lieutenant on 20 January 1944, his kills stood at 117 vehicles. In April he took command of 2nd Company, Heavy SS-Panzer Battalion 101.

The battalion (renumbered 501 in October 1944) was commanded by Lieutenant-Colonel von Westernhagen. It had a theoretical strength of forty-five Tigers, but actually numbered only thirty-seven, and fewer than half of them were available at Villers-Bocage; by 1 July only eleven were serviceable. At the time of the Allied invasion the battalion was stationed in the Beauvais area with Corps HQ at Septeuil west of Paris. It reached Normandy on 12 June and the 2nd Company found cover in a small wood north-east of Villers-Bocage, minus four tanks left with the workshop company under Lieutenant Stamm. The 1st Company, under Captain Mobius, deployed to their right.

On 13 June the Tigers planned to carry out routine maintenance until a British column was spotted outside Villers-Bocage. Wittmann decided to reconnoitre to the north-west towards Balleroy with four (possibly five) Tigers and one Panzer IV to clarify alarming reports that the British 7th Armoured Division had pushed into the left flank of Panzer Lehr. Fanning out, the panzers advanced on Villers-Bocage. Spotting the exposed British armoured column moving east towards Point 213, Wittmann realised that the road junction must be secured against the British.

At 0905 hours the lead elements of the 'Sharpshooters' and units of A Company reached Point 213. The main column of twenty-five vehicles stopped several hundred yards away on the hedge-lined highway, while most of the tanks, including four Cromwells and one Firefly, spread out to the north. Wittmann's gunlayer, Sergeant Balthasar Woll, who had served Wittmann well in Russia, and whose own tank was now under repair, grumbled, 'They're acting as if they've won the war already.' Wittmann replied, 'We're going to prove them wrong.'

Two or three of the Tigers were spotted running parallel to the column, but Wittmann to the north decided to circle round and attack without waiting for the others. Heading in from the east, he rammed aside a Cromwell that was blocking his way and drove into rue Clemenceau, the town's high street. In the town square the dismounted Regimental HQ's tank crews were surprised to be confronted by the lumbering Tiger tank. Any 6-pounder anti-tank guns that had been deployed were useless as their shells simply bounced off its thick armour.

First, Lieutenant Colonel Cranley's tank was knocked out. Regimental Second-in-Command Major Carr fired from point-blank range at the Tiger, but to no effect.

Another Tiger moving through Morgny. Note the haphazard nature of the sprayed-on camouflage scheme. (See colour plate 4.)

A Tiger I somewhere in Normandy. Again note the ripple effect camouflage that on this vehicle does not seem to extend to the wheels.

Wittmann's Tiger now halted as Carr's Cromwell exploded in flames, as did the regimental sergeant major's tank. The driver of the fourth tank, commanded by Captain Pat Dyas, reversed desperately out of the way into a garden, but Dyas himself and his gunner were both outside their tank and could only watch helplessly as the Tiger drove by, presenting its weaker side armour.

Wittmann then drove down towards the river valley of the Seulles past some bombed-out houses. At the road junction he bumped into Major Aird's B Squadron, parked on the Caumont road. Sergeant Stan Lockwood, commanding a Sherman Firefly, had heard all the firing and was now confronted by a scout car and its frantically waving driver. Lockwood drove round a corner to find Wittmann's Tiger side-on some 200 yards away, firing down a side street. The Firefly thumped four 17-pounder rounds into the Tiger, which caught fire, but its turret rotated and a shell brought down half a building on Lockwood's tank; when his crew emerged from the rubble the Tiger had vanished.

The Tiger beat a hasty retreat back up the hill, where it encountered Dyas's Cromwell. Wittmann's Tiger sustained two more hits before the Cromwell was brewed up and two of its crew killed. Lying to the left of and parallel to the highway was a narrow track, and as his Tiger clanked along this track Wittmann's first victim was a half-track vehicle at the base of the column. An unsuspecting Honey light tank was the next. Further up the road a 6-pounder crew hurriedly swung their gun round, but a well-placed shell hit the Bren carrier loaded with ammunition in front of it. Wittmann then proceeded to brew up the rest of the startled column, knocking out a row of Bren carriers and half-tracks as British armour-piercing shells bounced off his impervious armour. One tank commander courageously tried to block his path on the track, but the Tiger simply drove onto the road, mangling everything in his path.

Wittmann then withdrew to the woods to the southeast. In just five minutes he had reduced Cranley's advance to a burning shambles, destroying over twenty-five vehicles single-handedly. Frantically Dyas made contact with Major Aird and radioed Cranley to inform him what had happened. Cranley, in his last radio message, replied he also was under attack from German Tiger tanks and needed help.

In the early afternoon a triumphant Wittmann, his Tiger now rearmed and refuelled, returned to join the rest of his forces – four Tigers, the Mark IV and possibly three other tanks with infantry support – attacking the remnants of A Squadron and A Company, still trapped around Point 213. On the edge of the hill at least two Cromwells and one Firefly were knocked out, blocking the road, while not far away in the woods on the crown of the hill two more Cromwells were destroyed. Major Aird dispatched three Cromwells and a Firefly under Lieutenant Bill Cotton to try to make contact. They managed to cross the town, but were unable

One of the Tiger's victims in Villers-Bocage, a 7th Armoured Division Sherman knocked out on 13 June 1944.

The remains of a Sharpshooter's Cromwell tank in Villers-Bocage.

(*Above*) Michael Wittmann's burnt-out late model Tiger. (See colour plates 5 and 6..)

(*Opposite, top*) Another knocked-out Tiger in the rubble of Villers-Bocage. Wittmann's tank is visible in the background. The RAF flattened the town after the battle.

(*Opposite, below*) A well camouflaged Tiger from Heavy SS-Panzer Battalion 101 photographed just after the engagement at Villers-Bocage.

Another Cromwell tank that fell victim to Wittmann's Tiger.

to get over the railway embankment and turned back to take up positions in the town square.

The survivors of A Squadron were quickly overrun by Wittmann's forces, and Cranley and many of his men were captured. The Sharpshooters lost four men killed, five wounded and seventy-six missing, while at least twenty Cromwells, four Fireflys, three Honeys, three scout cars and a half-track were destroyed. A Company lost eighty men, including three officers, while about thirty infantry managed to escape. This left only B Squadron precariously holding on in Villers-Bocage.

Villers-Bocage was just a foretaste of things to come when it came to the Tiger's tank-killing capabilities. Heavy SS-Panzer Battalion 102, supported by panzer-grenadiers from the 9th SS Panzer Division, attacked Canadian positions at Hill 112 on 10 July. The battalion first went into action at Maltot to the north-east of the hill, when four Tigers securing the flank knocked out three Shermans while another Sherman fled in the direction of Eterville. Fourteen Tiger tanks then struck toward St Martin to the south-east of Hill 112 and were met by Shermans, which poured fire into the leading Tiger.

German platoon commander Will Fey recalled the attack:

Three enemy tanks were already silenced; the others kept on firing without pause. Then we finally had the most eager one in our crosshairs. The two furthest to our right had already been knocked out by us with five anti-tank shells, when light bombers showed up above the battleground. Like eagles, they fell out of the sky, dropped their loads of bombs, pulled up, and climbed away again. They came at us like a swarm of hostile hornets and covered us with a hail of medium bombs. At the same time, smoke shells landed among us and covered everything around with an impenetrable white fog within minutes. This was a new way of fighting to us, something we had not encountered on any battleground before. We withdrew to the starting positions where at least the infantry were able to keep the enemy close-assault teams away from us.

The attack was renewed the following day, but an artillery barrage greeted the Tigers, though they managed to knock out a few Churchill tanks. A smokescreen then descended on the panzers and Fey's tank took several hits to the rear and the turret, before stumbling upon enemy trucks and personnel carriers. Two Churchills were quickly knocked out. By the evening the Tigers had secured Hill 112, which would be fought over until the end of the month, when the Germans finally gave up its scorched earth. In the meantime it would change hands repeatedly.

The one tank capable of taking on the Tiger was the Sherman Firefly, armed with the British 17-pounder anti-tank gun.

(*Above*) A Tiger knocked out in Normandy. It appears to have caught fire, judging by the scorch marks.

(*Opposite, top*) A towed 17-pounder anti-tank gun; the tractor is a Morris C8. This gun could penetrate 231mm of armour at 1,000 yards.

(*Opposite, below*) A selection of 17-pounder ammunition, giving some impression of the size of the rounds. On the left is a wooden drill round.

During the night of the 11th the British moved back on to the hill and the isolated Tigers withdrew to St Martin. Two days later they attacked again, recapturing the wooded area of the cattle pen on the summit. An Allied bombardment ensured that the supporting panzergrenadiers could not remain there and on the 15th the Tigers once again found themselves alone amid the shattered landscape. The following morning the 10th SS came to their assistance.

When the Canadians occupied Matlot, some Tigers were sent to clear them out. They were met by a deluge of artillery fire but caught a column of four Churchill tanks on the road, knocking out the first and last vehicles. The two tanks in the middle were caught trying desperately to escape down the embankment; the last one was hit twice in the rear. Anti-tank guns and fighter-bombers then attacked the Tigers. Despite advancing beyond Matlot, Will Fey and his comrades were then recalled to their original positions.

On 24 July the Tigers intercepted eight Churchills striking from Matlot toward St Martin; none escaped. The next day the Tigers were bombed when a raid covered Hill 112 all the way back to St Martin. Fey and his comrades were then relieved by the 3rd Company and withdrew, only to be thrown into the fight again on the 26th around Hill 67 and the northern exit of St Andre to the west of Feuguerolles.

In the fighting that followed, the Tiger next to Fey's tank was hit. Smoke poured from its hatches as the uninjured members of the crew sought to escape. Fey witnessed the carnage:

> The driver of the knocked-out Panzer wildly waved the bloody stump of his arm, from which his hand was dangling, held by some pieces of skin and flesh, and sought cover with the other survivors to the side. The radio operator had been killed by a direct hit. Our other Panzers then advanced from their standby positions to the ridge of the hills. Across from us, there was no more movement. Everything remained quiet.

On 1 August Heavy SS-Panzer Battalion 102 was ordered to withdraw south under cover of darkness to assist the 9th SS Panzer Division, which was involved in heavy fighting with British and Canadian armoured forces. Arriving in Vire, they found the place reduced to rubble by air attacks. They then moved north to assist German paratroops under attack along the railway embankment. The following day elements of the battalion, along with the weak reconnaissance battalion from the 10th SS and a company of paratroops, were ordered to counterattack north of Vire.

In the initial engagement the Tigers knocked out five Cromwell tanks. They then bumped into concealed Shermans, but these were also swiftly dealt with. In total, twenty-two tanks belonging to the British Guards Armoured Division were knocked out without any loss. The following day the battalion continued to take its toll on the

A Tiger from Heavy Panzer Battalion 503 on the retreat; those that escaped the Allies ended up abandoned on the docks at Rouen.

An intriguing shot of a late production Tiger that has been incorporated into someone's wood pile. Judging by the broken track, this tank was disabled. Camouflage markings and the German cross can be seen on the side.

(*Above*) The fate of all the Tigers in Normandy – knocked out or simply abandoned.

(*Opposite, top*) At least three functioning Tigers were abandoned on Rouen docks; panzertruppen later slipped back across the Seine and blew them up.

(*Opposite, below*) This Canadian soldier is giving some idea of the width of the Tiger's off-road tracks.

British tanks. At 2300 on 3 August they withdrew, claiming twenty-eight enemy tanks and fourteen trucks destroyed, and two armoured scout cars and two motorbikes captured.

The Tigers had helped halt the Guards Armoured Division near Estry and stopped the 11th Armoured Division's push toward the Vire–Vassy Road. North-west of Vassy on 7 August the Tigers halted a massed armoured column with devastating effect: opening fire at just 400 metres, they knocked out fourteen of the fifteen attacking Shermans, along with numerous other vehicles. It was carnage.

The next day ten tanks of the 101st, supporting Kampfgruppe Waldmüller, were thrown into action against Operation Totalise, the Allied attempt to break through to Falaise. The juggernaut of the 1st Polish Armoured and 4th Canadian Armoured Divisions were poised to roll.

Colonel Kurt Meyer later recalled: 'Once more I shake Michael Wittmann's hand and refer to the extremely critical situation. Our good Michael laughs his boyish laughter and climbs into his Tiger. So far, 138 enemy tanks in the East and West have fallen victim to him. Will he be able to increase this number of successes or become a victim himself?'

The Tigers, with the grenadiers behind them, struck towards the wood south-east of Carcelles, where the Allied tanks were assembled. A massive Allied air raid in support of their offensive failed to hit a single panzer. However, it was at this point that Wittmann's luck ran out. Captain Wolfgang Rabe MD, Heavy SS-Panzer Battalion 101's physician, reported:

> Wittmann was east of the road to Caen with four or five Tigers. I was off to the side. The panzers came under fire, reportedly from English 15cm guns. Some of the Tigers went up in flames. I tried to determine if anyone got out. When I did not see anybody, I thought they might have left the panzer through the lower hatch and I tried to get closer. This was impossible since I came under fire as soon as I left the ditch in an easterly direction. We waited another hour or two for any of the crews to show up. Towards evening I drove over to Brigadeführer Kraemer, Chief of the General Staff, I SS Panzer Corps, and reported on developments. He ordered me, since I was the senior officer of the battalion, to lead the remains of the battalion back, and attached me to SS-Panzer Regiment 12.

Other reports stated that Wittmann succumbed to British Shermans and a Typhoon rocket attack. At the time of his death he was credited not only with destroying 138 AFVs, most of them tanks, but also with 132 anti-tank gun kills, all of which he had chalked up in less than two years.

Chapter Eight

Tiger II:
Normandy to Berlin

Tiger IIs first saw action with the 1st Company, Heavy Panzer Battalion 503, during the battle of Normandy, when they were used to counter Operation Atlantic between Troarn and Demouville on 18 July 1944. Two tanks were lost in action, while the company commander's tank got stuck in a bomb crater that had been created during Operation Goodwood. In the Cagny sector south-east of Caen the Germans knocked out forty Allied tanks, with the 503rd accounting for the bulk of them.

The battalion's 3rd Company, having lost all its Tiger Is, was sent to the training ground at Mailly-le-Camp in eastern France, north of Troyes, to covert to the Tiger II. On 12 August, en route to the front, their train was attacked by fighter–bombers between Sézanne and Esternay, and most of the tanks were wrecked. One of the last remaining Tiger IIs in Normandy was abandoned by its crew while under tow by a Bergepanther near Vimoutiers on 2 August 1944. As so few Tiger IIs were engaged in Normandy (about a dozen in total) it is difficult to assess their effectiveness.

The survivors of Heavy SS-Panzer Battalion 501 (formerly 101), 502 (formerly 102) and 503, having blown up the last of their Tiger tanks in Normandy, were shipped back to Germany. In early September the battalions were gathered at Paderborn. The latter two battalions were destined to fight in Hungary, East Prussia and Berlin in the closing months of the war, while the 501st would be involved in Hitler's last futile offensive in Hungary.

Heavy SS-Panzer Battalion 502 was refitted at Sennelager, while the 503rd's 1st Company moved to Bentfeld, the 2nd to Eilsen and the 3rd to Hovelhof. Panzer Training and Replacement Battalion 500 at Paderborn provided much-needed crews and between 19 and 22 September the 503rd received forty-five new Tiger IIs. The following month the unit was shipped to Hungary as part of the Feldhernhalle Panzer Corps and assisted in the futile defence of Budapest.

The Tiger II's debut on the Eastern Front did not go terribly well. Elements of Heavy SS-Panzer Battalion 501 first went into battle with the Tiger II on 12 August

An abandoned Tiger II of Heavy Panzer Battalion 503 near Vimoutiers on 22 August 1944. Its fleeing crew probably set it on fire. (This tank is also shown on pp. 34, 35 and 36.)

1944 in the face of the Soviet Lvov–Sandomierz offensive near Baranów. In this action a single Soviet T-34/85 from the 53rd Guards Tank Brigade, under Guards Lieutenant Os'kin, knocked out three Tiger IIs by hitting their side armour from an ambush position. In addition, eleven IS-2 heavy tanks of the Soviet 71st Heavy Tank Regiment took on fourteen Tiger IIs, knocking out four and damaging another seven, for the loss of three IS-2s.

Those Tiger IIs captured near Sandomierz were soon tested by the Soviets at Kubinka. The range trials revealed that they were less of a threat than the much lighter and cheaper Tiger I, and the Soviets were puzzled at the German decision to produce it. Tests showed that the transmission and suspension broke down regularly and the engine was likely to overheat. They also discovered surprising deficiencies in the Tiger II's armour: not only was the metal of poor quality, so was the welding. As a result, even when shells did not penetrate the armour, there was a large amount of spalling, and when struck by heavier shells the armour plating cracked at the welds.

Some two months later, on 15 October 1944, Tiger IIs of Heavy Panzer Battalion 503 were involved in Operation Panzerfaust, during which Otto Skorzeny seized Budapest to stop Hungary defecting to the Soviet camp. In the subsequent fighting in Hungary the battalion accounted for 121 Soviet tanks, 244 anti-tank guns and artillery pieces, five aircraft and a train! The 503rd lost twenty-five Tiger IIs: ten were knocked out and caught fire, thirteen were destroyed by their own crews to prevent them from falling into enemy hands and two were sent back to Vienna to be overhauled.

In August 1943 Heavy Panzer Battalion 506, which had been fighting on the Eastern Front with Tiger Is, was also withdrawn to Germany and refitted with Tiger IIs, and was subsequently involved in the resistance to Operation Market Garden. Major Winrich Behr, serving with General Krebs, Field Marshal Model's Chief of Staff, recalled that by mid-September

> [In the Netherlands] there was an enormous concentration of heavy armour in all stages of preparation, from cannibalised wrecks to fully battle-ready Tigers. Some of these were the updated Royal Tigers, with much thicker armour-plating and larger guns, which had proved a match for the Russian T-34s. Among its armament was the 8.8cm gun (originally an anti-aircraft weapon) that had wrought such havoc among the British tanks in North Africa.

Heavy Tank Battalion 506 consisted of some sixty powerful Tiger IIs. In support of the 9th SS Panzer Division, it set about eliminating the British paratroops trapped at Oosterbeek during mid-September 1944. Luckily for the paras, these attacks were not very well coordinated. When the 10th SS was eventually forced back, forty-five Tigers and a company of Panthers were sent to reinforce them, following the landing of the Polish 1st Parachute Brigade at Driel, south of Oosterbeek.

The 506th, reinforced by a company of Tiger Is, was the only German Army Tiger unit to take part in Hitler's Ardennes offensive. At 0530 on Saturday, 16 December 1944 2,000 German guns heralded a surprise German offensive on the Western Front. For the next five weeks the panzers fought a desperate struggle to reach Brussels and Antwerp, in what became known as the Battle of the Bulge.

About 150 Tiger Is and IIs fought in the Ardennes, deployed in their individual heavy tank battalions supporting the panzer and SS panzer divisions, but they were unable to achieve much during the hard-fought battle. Key among them was Heavy SS-Panzer Battalion 501, assigned to Kampfgruppe Peiper, whose Tiger IIs led the attack in the north. Five Ferdinands also fought to the south of Bastogne, arriving in time to help cover the German withdrawal.

The battalion was filmed passing through Tondorf on its way to Kampfgruppe Peiper's assembly area and the Tiger IIs certainly looked an imposing and formidable

(*Above*) Allied Supreme Commander General Dwight D. Eisenhower inspects a flipped Tiger II in the Falaise pocket.

(*Opposite, top*) Another Tiger II from Heavy Panzer Battalion 503, this time in Budapest in mid-October 1944 during Operation Panzerfaust. The two men standing on the later-type turret are Hungarian soldiers.

(*Opposite, below*) A close-up of the very large mantlet on the improved Henschel/Wegmann turret.

The presence of the 503rd's Tiger IIs on the streets of Budapest helped ensure Hungarian loyalty to Hitler's cause.

fighting force. Even so, the tanks were still dwarfed by the houses that lined the narrow streets. They were clear of external storage, though the turrets had been reinforced with the addition of spare track links. The crews looked quietly confident, but they were posing for the camera.

The Tigers were later photographed at Deidenberg and Kaiserbarracke carrying German paratroops and these images came to epitomise Hitler's powerful Ardennes thrust. They were a symbol of his revived military power with elite troops borne by his very latest panzers; the reality of the battle was to prove somewhat different. The Tiger IIs were never to be assigned the Durchbruchwagen role originally envisaged for the Tiger.

Overall, Peiper's weak panzer regiment numbered around twenty Tiger IIs, as well as thirty-five Panthers and thirty-five Panzer IVs. As the offensive was essentially a race against time, Peiper saw his battalion of cumbersome Tiger IIs as much less valuable than his Panzer IVs and Panthers. He deployed them at the rear of his attack column, ready to be called forward once they reached the open countryside near the River Meuse. He was being wildly optimistic if he really thought they were ever going to get that far. The road from Ligneuville to Stavelot was, in Peiper's words, suitable for little more than bicycles. In addition, getting the heavy tanks over the Amblève and Salm rivers proved to be a major problem after the Americans blew up several bridges.

During the early hours of 19 December, masked by dense fog, Peiper's forces attacked Stoumont, west of La Gleize, which was defended by American infantry supported by towed anti-tank guns. They also had two 90mm anti-aircraft guns, which had only just arrived from America. Unfortunately one gun ended up stuck in a ditch. Under the covering fog and early morning darkness two Tigers and two Panthers approached the town. Half the panzers were immediately caught in the rear by American Bazooka fire and began to burn. One of the surviving Tigers then ran into the remaining 90mm gun: the first round hit its front left sprocket and the second took off most of the gun barrel. The crew fled. Later in the day American reinforcements, including Shermans and an M36 tank destroyer armed with a 90mm gun, blocked Peiper's advance at Stoumont station. The M36 tank destroyer had only entered service in late 1944 and proved very successful against the Tiger at long range.

Thwarted at Trois-Ponts by 21 December, Peiper was holding a defensive position around La Gleize. The half dozen Tiger IIs with his force were deployed on the south-eastern and north-eastern approaches, where they had good fields of fire. However, they soon succumbed to heavy bombardment from American artillery and counterattacks by the US 3rd Armored Division. By the end of the day half the Tigers were out of action. Although another half-dozen operational Tiger IIs were east of Peiper at Stavelot, they were unable to get to him as the bridge over the Amblève was down. Tiger 222 was hit by the Americans and abandoned on the southern end of Stavelot Bridge on the 19th. Two more were hit in the rear in the narrow streets.

By 24 December Peiper's battle group had ceased to exist. Tiger 008 had the dubious accolade of being the last operational panzer still on the northern bank of the Amblève between Stavelot and Trois-Ponts. Although the tank carried on fighting, it had been immobilised by mechanical trouble. Its crew set it on fire east of Petit-Spai near La Ferme Antoine on Christmas day.

Peiper left seven Tiger IIs in or near La Gleize. Among them was Tiger 204, which the Americans tried to drive to the railway station at Spa; sporting a precautionary white flag, it got as far as Ruy before breaking down. Tiger 213 was found in a field near Wérimont Farm at La Gleize and, after restoration, was eventually placed in front of La Gleize Museum.

On Christmas day Tiger 332, heading for Peiper's abandoned positions, was caught by a Sherman firing phosphorus. The crew, thinking their tank was on fire, baled out. Tiger 332 was eventually shipped to America. Another three Tigers were left at Stavelot. So ended the Tiger II's less than glorious participation in the Ardennes offensive. Under less-than-favourable conditions, its role as a breakthrough tank had ended in failure.

After taking part in Hitler's ill-fated Ardennes offensive in December 1944, the mighty Tiger II was also involved in the last major offensive of the war on the Eastern Front. Heavy Panzer Battalion 503, having refitted with Tiger IIs in France, and after fighting in Normandy, moved into Hungary. Similarly the 509th refitted with Tiger IIs in Germany in late 1944 and moved into Hungary in January 1945.

By January 1945 Heavy Panzer Battalion 503 was back in Germany to take part in one of Hitler's last ill-fated counterattacks. It was split in two, with one group sent to the Arnswalde-Pomerania area and the other to the Landsberg-Kustrin area. The first group, under Lieutenant Colonel Fritz Herzig, along with a panzer support battalion, became trapped in Arnswalde on 4 February. Herzig's Tiger II could easily have broken out but that would have meant abandoning everyone else to their fate at the hands of the Russians. Three days later Second Lieutenant Fritz Kauerauf with three Tiger IIs set out from Stargard for Arsnwalde via Reetz. Instead, he became involved with the 11th SS trying to stop the Russian advance to the Baltic.

Initially they made good progress on the first day of the attack, penetrating the Russian envelopment of Arnswalde and rescuing the German garrison. The 503's Tiger IIs were instrumental in holding open the corridor as the wounded and civilians were evacuated and fresh troops sent in. During the fighting in the Danzig-Gotenhafen area Tigers of the 503rd destroyed sixty-four Soviet tanks. However, the 10th SS and 503rd's success was short-lived. The Tigers could do little once the 2nd Soviet Guards Tank Army brought up its heavy Joseph Stalin tanks.

A German and a Hungarian share a cigarette next to the imposing bulk of the Tiger II.

This Tiger is preparing to take part in Hitler's ill-fated counteroffensive against the Red Army in Hungary.

This Tiger was captured by the Red Army in the summer of 1944.

A Tiger II of Heavy SS-Panzer Battalion 501 passing through Tondorf to the Kampfgruppe Peiper assembly areas prior to the Ardennes offensive.

To the south the 60th Panzergrenadier Division Feldherrnhalle, with a handful of Tiger IIs, the 13th Panzer Division and the 9th SS Corps (8th SS and 22nd SS Kavallerie Divisions) were trapped in the Hungarian capital Budapest, while the 18th SS Panzergrenadier Division was forced to retreat. In the bitter fighting for the city the Tiger IIs were to become little more than glorified pillboxes.

Hitler wanted to strike between Lake Balaton and Lake Velencze, south-west of Budapest, in an operation dubbed Operation Spring Awakening. He believed that if the Soviets were caught by surprise, they could be thrown back. The 6th SS Panzer Army fielded two heavy tank battalions equipped with about sixty Tiger IIs. On the morning of 6 March 1945, after a 30-minute artillery bombardment supported by air attacks, the Germans crashed into the Soviet defences. The deployment of the mighty Tiger IIs proved a disaster: there was no frost and the mud immediately claimed fifteen tanks that sank up to their turrets. Wherever the remaining Tiger IIs went, they dealt with their opponents with impunity, but they were heavy, mechanically unreliable and never available in sufficient numbers to stem the tide.

Tiger 204 near Ruy, having been salvaged by the Americans from La Gleize following the destruction of Kampfgruppe Peiper.

The triumphant crew of an M10 tank-destroyer responsible for killing four Tigers at Stavelot.

This Tiger in the northern sector of the Ardennes front was probably caught by Allied fighter-bombers.

American troops on Tiger 312, which was knocked out during the Battle of the Bulge.

Heavy Panzer Battalion 503 had been issued with thirty-six Tiger IIs in February 1945; by mid-March it had just ten, which were moved to defend the Oder. Six Tiger IIs of the 503rd were involved in Berlin's final death throes. From January to April 1945 the 503rd claimed 500 enemy tanks destroyed for the loss of forty-five Tiger IIs, most of which were abandoned after breaking down. On 18 April they knocked out sixty-four Russian tanks for the loss of one Tiger, before withdrawing on the German capital. Five were still operational by 1 May; they attempted to break out during the night, but did not get far. After destroying thirty-nine Russian tanks on the streets of Berlin, the last Tiger II was blown up by its crew.

Heavy Panzer Battalion 502 fared little better. On 5 January 1945 it was renumbered 511, and on 31 March 1945 the crews of 3rd Company, Battalions 510 and 511, collected the last thirteen Tiger IIs directly from the Henschel factory. They

Tiger 332 being prepared for its journey to America.

The Tiger IIs did not fare well in the confines of the Ardennes and failed in their breakthrough role.

Another turretless Tiger II bears testimony to its failure in the Battle of the Bulge.

also received three second-hand Tiger IIs from the Waffenamt at Sennelager and one from Northeim.

The delay in the delivery of Tiger IIs to Battalion 502 due to heavy air attacks on the Henschel plant in Kassel meant that the battalion did not move to the Oder between Frankfurt and Kustrin until early March and then only with twenty-nine tanks. They were thrown into the attack near Sachsenheim; the Russians fell back and the Tigers soon outstripped the other panzers in pursuit. On 26/27 March, involved in an attempt to break through to Kustrin, the unit ended its days with the 9th Army in the Halbe pocket.

Panzer driver Lance Corporal Lothar Tiby witnessed the end of the Tigers on 2 May 1945:

> The heavy fighting against a vastly superior force lasted all day. There were very high losses of vehicles, infantry and civilians on our side and very high losses of personnel carriers and infantry on the Russian side due to the action of the two Panzers. During a renewed attempt to break through, Schafer's Panzer took a direct hit, two men dead, the rest seriously wounded. A further attempt to break out was no longer possible. Our vehicle, the last Panzer of the battalion, was destroyed.

Chapter Nine

Tiger Tales

What of the men who fought in the Tiger? Well, they produced a particularly tough breed of panzer ace. Their thick armour and long range enabled both Tiger Is and IIs to stay in the fight that much longer than ordinary tanks. The heavy tank battalions produced at least twenty-eight of the top tank-killers, who accounted for some 2,500 tanks, though not all these kills were achieved using just the Tiger. Key among these aces were Kurt Knispel, Johannes Bälter, Otto Carius, Martin Schroif and Michael Wittmann, who knocked out well over a hundred tanks apiece. Bälter, who served with Heavy Panzer Battalion 502, was variously credited with 139 or 144 kills during the war.

When the Tigers were committed in Tunisia, the realities of war soon struck home with the crews. The fighting conditions proved far from ideal, and the men were thankful for the tank's thick armour. Major Lueder, who commanded the advance element of the 501st, recorded that committing the Tiger to close-quarter combat did not play to its strengths. The Tiger lost its stand-off fighting advantage and the officers had to expose themselves to see what was going on.

In his combat report dated 18 December 1942 he recounted:

After being assigned security areas, the Tigers moved to an assembly area 7 kilometres east of Djedeida. The order to attack came at 13.00 hours and the Panzers immediately started toward Djedeida to gain contact with the oncoming enemy tank force moving northwestwards. At 15:00 the Panzers encountered first enemy activity, weak infantry forces 3 kilometres northwest of Djedeida. The Company was hit by heavy artillery fire from the heights north of Tebourba and also repeatedly attacked by strafing aircraft. Captain Baron von Nolde fell when an artillery shell exploded when he was walking toward a Tiger.

The attack was carried forward against enemy tanks in the olive groves 5 kilometres west of Djedeida. The field of view and the field of fire were very limited by the thick olive groves. Enemy tanks could only be fought at close range. Captain Deichmann, who left his Panzer to obtain a better view, was hit in the stomach by a rifle shot. The Tigers were hit by General Lee tanks firing at a range of 80 to 100 metres. This resulted in deep penetrations, but the last 10mm of side armour held. This proved that the armour is excellent.

Two General Lee tanks were knocked out at a range of 150 metres. Others were eliminated by 88mm flak guns. The rest pulled back.

In summing up the lessons learned from this encounter, Lueder noted:

> Although it was undesirable to send only a few Tigers into action, this was necessary due to the enemy situation and the shortage of our own forces. The approach march was engaged by long-range enemy artillery fire that could not be suppressed.
>
> It is especially difficult to direct Panzers in combat in olive groves because the thick tree crowns take away the commander's and gunner's view. An attacking panzer is easily knocked out by well sited dug-in defences.
>
> In spite of unfavourable conditions, the crews' trust in their Tigers has greatly increased because of the quality of the armour.

Despite the Tiger's long-range killing power, the panzertruppen had mixed views. For example, tank ace Colonel Franz Bäke, a hardened veteran of the 6th Panzer Division, said, 'I preferred the Panther to the Tiger, although it, too, was an outstanding combat vehicle.' He felt that the Panther had the edge when it came to firepower, rate of fire and speed, adding, 'If we had had this Panther in 1941, the Army would have rolled straight to Moscow.'

Bäke proved himself an outstanding panzer commander on the Eastern Front, rising to take command of 5th Panzer's 11th Panzer Regiment in mid-1943. His particular claim to fame was as the leader of Heavy Panzer Regiment Bäke, which included both Tigers and Panthers. While Bäke himself fought in the Panther, this duality placed him in an ideal position to judge the merits of both tanks in the fiercest of combat conditions. This was particularly so during the brutal battle for the Cherkassy pocket.

In January 1944 Bäke found that, in addition to the 11th Panzer Regiment, thirty-four Tigers of Heavy Panzer Battalion 503 and forty-seven Panthers of the 2nd Battalion, 23rd Panzer Regiment, had been placed under his command. Supported by 150mm Hummel self-propelled guns of the 1st Battalion, 88th Artillery Regiment, this powerful grouping became Heavy Panzer Regiment Bäke. The unit's role was to try to help shore up the situation in the Ukraine following repeated Soviet attacks.

In beating back the Soviet 3rd Tank Corps, Bäke's Tigers and Panthers knocked out 268 Soviet tanks and assault guns. They also overran or destroyed 156 enemy gun positions. The following month, from 4 to 8 February 1944, eleven Tigers and fourteen Panthers from Heavy Panzer Regiment Bäke were involved in the effort to

A Soviet sentry stands guard over a captured Ferdinand. No damage is visible and it seems to be in a hull-down position. (This tank is also shown on p. 50.)

free the troops trapped in the Cherkassy pocket. Their first attempt failed, so Bäke then struck from the Ruban–Most area employing three armoured assault groups.

His well rehearsed tactics involved the Panthers charging forwards on the flanks while the Tigers followed up about 300 metres behind in the centre. As soon as the enemy opened fire, the Tigers were able to silence them and in the meantime the Panthers had outflanked the Soviet anti-tank guns. As soon as the Soviet gunners and tankers broke cover, the Tigers took them out at ranges of up to 2,000 metres.

Bäke's men accounted for eighty enemy tanks and assault guns. As usual, though, the Tigers and Panthers could do little in the face of overwhelming enemy numbers. By 13 February Bäke had only four operational Panthers. Field Marshal von Manstein sent him a message, 'Bravo! You have accomplished much, despite mud and the Russians. Now you must take the last step! Grit your teeth and have at them! This, too, will succeed!'

Reinforced by tanks sent forwards from the maintenance depots, Heavy Panzer Regiment Bäke and the 1st Panzer Division resumed the relief effort on 15 February. In the early hours of the following day they reached the Cherkassy pocket, enabling 35,000 men to escape.

The following month Heavy Panzer Regiment Bäke was reorganised as Panzer Group Bäke, which comprised the 2nd Battalion, 11th Panzer Regiment, the 6th Company, 1st Panzer Regiment, and the Tigers of Heavy Panzer Battalion 509. They were tasked with reopening the north–south route in the area of Stary Konstantinow. The Tigers under Captain König arrived at 2300 hours on 5 March

This Soviet officer seems to be making a technical evaluation of this knocked-out mid-production Tiger I.

Another mid-production example, Tiger 217 has been whitewashed for winter combat.

1944 and commenced their attack southwest on the right wing of the 11th Panzer Regiment the following morning. Despite resistance from enemy tanks, they reached the village of Kusmin at midday. A counterattack by Soviet T-34s near Kusmin was swiftly dealt with.

Shortly afterwards, on 10 March, the Soviets launched a major offensive against the boundary of the 1st Panzer Army and 8th Army southeast of Vinnitsa, and the Tigers were redeployed beyond the Bozok River to hold the line. Two days later Heavy Panzer Battalion 509 was the last unit to cross the river, knocking out two T-34s as it did so. Panzer Group Bäke withdrew on 16 March, by which time it consisted of twelve Tigers with elements from the 1st and 11th Panzer Regiments. Gathering at Proskurow, Bäke was instructed to re-establish contact with the 4th Panzer Army. This was no easy feat, linking two entire panzer armies!

The Tigers leading the charge attempted to break through to the developing Kamenets–Podolsk pocket. Fighting their way 30 kilometres west of Proskurow, they finally made contact with the 4th Panzer Army when they reached elements of the 1st SS Panzer Division. On 18 March, after receiving extra Tigers, Bäke's reinforced regiment attacked Dselintsche, destroying twelve Soviet assault guns, forty-four tanks including four heavy KV-1s and KV-85s, thirty-three anti-tank guns and a number of artillery pieces. The following day four Tigers, seven Panthers and seven assault guns, supported by ten armoured personnel carriers, reached Hill 349. The Soviets were ready for them this time and all the Tigers and three of the Panthers were disabled.

Time was now running out for Bäke's command. His forces were reduced to two Tigers, two Panthers, four Panzer IVs and four assault guns. In the face of overwhelming numbers, on 20 March his survivors were forced to withdraw, covered by the two Tiger tanks and four other stragglers. Salvageable Tigers were moved to the maintenance depot at Jaromolintsy to be repaired and Captain Murmester arrived to take charge of Heavy Panzer Battalion 509. On 23 March Colonel Franz Bäke was flown to the Führer's Headquarters to receive the Swords to the Knight's Cross with Oak Leaves from Hitler. The 509th, re-equipped with Tiger IIs, spent its final days defending Budapest and the survivors eventually surrendered to the Americans in Austria.

Another unit that achieved incredible success with the Tiger was the Grossdeutschland Panzergrenadier Regiment. Following the success of its Tiger tank company, the division formed an entire battalion equipped with forty-five Tigers. This unit went into action in August 1943 and fought on the Eastern Front until its surrender in East Prussia in 1945. In that time it clocked up the highest number of victories of any of the German Army's Tiger units, amounting to 1,036 Soviet tanks and other armoured fighting vehicles and over 300 guns.

Kurt Knispel was an panzer ace who had the distinction of serving in almost every type of panzer as a loader, gunner and commander on the Eastern Front. His

These mid-production Tigers, again in a winter whitewash, appear to have been abandoned.

An American soldier posing by a Jagdtiger. The top of the turret has been blown off.

Three rounds went through the back of this Sturmtiger, destroying the engine. It has also thrown a track.

total of 168 enemy tanks destroyed made him the top panzer ace of the war. He gained the Iron Cross, First Class after destroying his fiftieth enemy tank; he then gained the Gold Tank Assault badge after taking part in over a hundred tank battles. After Knispel destroyed 126 tanks (with a further twenty unconfirmed kills), he was awarded the German Cross in Gold. As commander of a Tiger I and then a Tiger II, he knocked out another forty-two enemy tanks. It was as a Tiger I gunner that he was able to truly demonstrate the tank's destructive capabilities in head- on battles with the T-34 tank. He excelled at gunnery from great distances and while on the move; coupled with the Tiger's high survivability, this made him a deadly adversary.

In October 1940 Knispel joined the 12th Panzer Division as a Panzer IV gunner. Three years later, credited with twelve kills, he became familiar with the Tiger I. He and a group of fellow panzertruppen were sent to Panzer Battalion 500 at Paderborn, where they were destined to become the 1st Company, Heavy Panzer Battalion 503.

By April 1943 he was serving with the 1st Company, Heavy Panzer Battalion 503, in a Tiger I named *Max*. This battalion was the first to reach its full authorised strength of three companies equipped with forty-five Tigers. However, for the Kursk offensive their strength was initially frittered away when the companies were allocated to three different divisions. Knispel's company was assigned to the 7th Panzer Division and advanced with them on the morning of 5 July 1943.

Soviet artillery had brought down the bridge over the Donets and they were unable to cross until mid-afternoon. By the third day only four of the 1st Company's twelve tanks were still operational. The first tank that Gunner Knispel destroyed was a T-34, his 88mm shell easily piercing the Soviet tank's frontal armour. It was at this point that the battalion was brought back together, forming part of a panzer wedge 40 kilometres wide. On day four of the battle Knispel knocked out another seven Soviet tanks.

In the confusion of the battle, he and his comrades passed fourteen Soviet tanks roaring in the opposite direction. Knispel and his crew gave chase, shooting up the Soviet tanks from behind. When three T-34s turned round to give battle, they were destroyed by a supporting Tiger.

On the last day of the attack the cry went up, 'Three o'clock, 800 metres – enemy tanks!'

'How many, Kurt?' cried tank commander Rippl, call sign 'Max'.

'About ten,' warned Knispel.

'Max to Moritz: we have a few tanks for you. Move towards us.'

'Moritz to Max,' replied tank commander Rubbel, 'we're coming.'

Knispel called 'Halt!'

He then fired and took off a T-34's turret.

'Direct hit!' shouted Rippl.

Knispel and his loader were hard at work destroying two more Soviet tanks.

'Max to Moritz, we have three.'

'Moritz to Max, leave some for us!'

Knispel accounted for another two T-34s, while Rubbel's Tiger also claimed two. As the remaining Soviet tanks turned and fled, Knispel hit another tank at 2,000 metres.

Knispel's battalion reached the Belgorod–Kursk main road on 14 July 1943 with just ten operational Tigers. This was where the main assault had commenced ten days earlier. The remaining Tigers now spent much of their time rescuing trapped German units. Despite their defeat at Kursk, Knispel had sealed his reputation. The battalion then began a steady retreat and by mid-August they were claiming the destruction of 385 tanks, four assault guns and 265 anti-tank guns since the start of Kursk. In January 1944 it became part of Heavy Panzer Regiment Bäke and later redeployed to Normandy with Tiger Is and IIs.

Even in the closing days of the war the Tiger II in the right hands achieved phenomenal results against quite remarkable odds. Karl Brommann joined the 6th SS Mountain Division at the start of the war. After being badly wounded, he was subsequently posted to the 11th SS Panzergrenadier Division. In October 1943 he transferred to Heavy SS-Panzer Battalion 103, equipped with Tiger Is. The following October his unit was issued with the Tiger II and moved to fight on the Eastern Front.

Fighting in the Stettin area, Brommann and his comrades helped cover the evacuation from East Prussia. In mid-February they were shipped by train to Danzig. During the fighting there, Brommann, in charge of the battalion's 2nd Company, exhibited some exemplary marksmanship by knocking out sixty-six Soviet tanks, forty-four anti-tank guns and fifteen other vehicles. This performance gained him the Knight's Cross. Wounded once more, he ended the war as a British PoW.

Similarly, Karl Körner joined Heavy SS-Panzer Battalion 103 in 1943 and shipped to the Eastern Front the following January. In the dying days of the Third Reich, Körner fought to defend Berlin. On the road between Bollersdorf and Strausberg his Tiger II ran into a Soviet brigade consisting of eleven Joseph Stalin tanks and up to 150 T-34/85s.

He attacked with two other Tiger IIs, catching the Soviets in the process of rearming and refuelling. The ammunition and fuel trucks exploded, causing panic among the Soviet crews. In the confusion Körner fired thirty-nine rounds and destroyed thirty-nine Soviet tanks before withdrawing to his own lines. Forced back on Berlin during the withdrawal, Körner and his crew hit 102 enemy tanks and twenty-six anti-tank guns. For this action he was awarded the Knight's Cross in the Führer bunker on 29 April 1945. He ended the war fighting in the Charlottenburg area.

While the likes of Bäke, Knispel and Wittman achieved great results with the Tiger, Otto Carius despaired of the Jagdtiger. The third highest scoring panzer ace, Carius was credited with knocking out over 150 tanks, most of these kills achieved with the Tiger I. He started the war serving with the 21st Panzer Regiment but transferred to Heavy Panzer Battalion 502 in 1943, fighting on the Leningrad front and around Narva.

After recovering from severe wounds sustained on 24 July 1944, he took command of the ten Jagdtigers that formed 2nd Company, Heavy Panzerjäger Battalion 512. This unit's track record was appalling. They managed to destroy just one American tank for the loss of one Jagdtiger in action. Eight others broke down and/or were subsequently destroyed by their crews, and one was knocked out by friendly fire.

Battalion 512's finest moment came on 9 April 1945 when the 1st Company managed to destroy eleven tanks and thirty other vehicles – a number of the enemy tanks were knocked out at 4,000 metres. The unit only lost one Jagdtiger and that

One of the few Soviet tanks capable of taking on a Tiger was the IS-2, armed with a massive 122mm gun.

A mid-production Tiger coated in Zimmerit paste.

was to an American fighter-bomber. The 1st Company managed to account for a further five Sherman tanks before surrendering at Iserlohn. Near Aueheim two Jagdtigers serving with 14th Corps were used to attack enemy-held bunkers during 17–18 January 1945. During this fighting an American Sherman was destroyed using high-explosive shells.

Otto Carius could find no fault with the destructive power of the massive 128mm anti-tank gun, which was capable of piercing a house and any tank lurking behind it. Deployed on the wide open spaces of the Russian steppes in a hull-down position, the Jagdtiger could have been deadly. Instead, deployed in the confines of the Ruhr industrial region, the Jagdtigers soon became trapped.

Carius complained that the gun had to be recalibrated every time the vehicle was taken off-road, thanks to the Porsche suspension. In addition, the gun had to be unlocked before firing, which meant one of his men had to climb out in the face of the enemy. On top of this, the ammunition came in two parts and required two loaders. This in turn meant the weapon had a very slow rate of fire. To turn the gun to face a target meant traversing the entire 72-ton vehicle, which caused the transmission and differentials to break down under the weight.

Despite all this, Carius observed that it was Allied air power combined with poor German crew training that prevented the Jagdtiger from achieving its full destructive

'Have trailer, will travel!' The US Army moves a captured Jagdtiger for closer inspection.

An early production Tiger I photographed by the US Army in the winter of 1944/45. It is in factory-sprayed dunkel gelb with blotches of white snow camouflage.

This Tiger II had its turret blown off in Normandy, thanks to the efforts of RAF Bomber Command. The same vehicle is shown on pp. 33.

In contrast, this Tiger II has had its gun barrel shot off.

American troops taking a closer look at the imposing bulk of the Jagdtiger.

An abandoned Tiger I and Panther bogged down in a sea of mud. These two panzer types worked well together.

potential. These factors naturally had a negative impact on the Jagdtiger crews, who were simply not prepared to stand their ground regardless of the thick armour and huge gun. With their training still incomplete on 8 March 1945, he and his men were sent to the front near Sieburg. During the fighting in the Ruhr pocket two well camouflaged Jagdtigers ignored an approaching American column for fear of provoking an air attack by Allied fighter-bombers. In their panic the crews tried to withdraw and both vehicles broke down.

Carius took great care preparing his positions on the high ground at Siegen, ready to ambush American tanks, only to be given away by local German civilians. Disastrously, the local home guard proceeded to knock out one of his strange-looking vehicles as they did not realise it was a panzer, while another one became trapped in a bomb crater.

Near Unna one Jagdtiger attempted to face off five American tanks, but once again inexperience told against the crew. After taking successive hits from three tanks at 600 metres, the Jagdtiger crew, instead of reversing away from the enemy, turned tail. As they did so, they exposed the thinner side armour and all the crew were killed by American tank fire. Trapped in the Ruhr pocket, having lost all their vehicles, Carius and his men eventually surrendered in Iserlohn.

Chapter Ten

Tiger Stalking

Allied tank crews had every reason to fear the Tiger; its 88mm gun was capable of chewing up every single opponent it faced. From a 30 degree angle it could pierce the front glacis plate of an American M4 Sherman at a range of between 1,800m and 2,100m, the British Churchill IV's between 1,100m and 1,700m, the Soviet T-34's between 800 and 1,400m and the Soviet IS-2's between 100m and 300m. Clearly taking on the Tiger with a Sherman or a T-34 was not a pleasant experience.

Allied tank guns required tankers to close to two-thirds to half the Tiger's range before they could engage. Neither the M4 Sherman's 75mm gun nor the T-34's 76.2mm gun could penetrate the Tiger's frontal armour at any range. However, the T-34 with the 85mm gun could tackle it between 200 and 500m and the IS-2 with its 122mm gun between 500 and 1,500m. Likewise the Soviet 100mm tank gun and the 152mm howitzer could take on the Tiger out to ranges of 1,000m. This meant that as the war progressed, the Soviets were increasingly able to keep the Tiger at arm's length.

The American 76mm gun, using certain types of armour-piercing shell, could penetrate a Tiger's armour at just over 500m. Only the later M36 Gun Motor Carriage and M26 heavy tank armed with the 90mm gun proved capable of knocking out the Tiger at long range. Much more successful was the British 17-pounder anti-tank gun that could tackle the Tiger out to 1,000m. As a towed anti-tank gun, this weapon was in short supply; equally, British armour armed with it – the Sherman Firefly, Challenger, Comet, Achilles and Archer – were too few in number and too lightly armoured. The Sherman Firefly was the only Allied tank committed to the D-Day landings that could take on the Tiger and Panther on anything like equal terms.

The 17-pounder was by far the best anti-tank gun possessed by the British Army towards the end of the Second World War and was a real tank-killer capable of penetrating up to 231mm armour at 1,000 metres, and as a result it was employed in a variety of guises. The British Army went to war in 1939 with wholly inadequate anti-tank guns, principally the 2-pounder (40mm) developed in the mid-1930s and the 6-pounder (57mm) developed in the late 1930s, though the latter did not enter production until 1941 because the War Office insisted on replacing those 2-pounders lost in France. These weapons were quickly outgunned by the German 50mm and 75mm guns.

By early 1942 prototypes of a 3in (76mm) weapon firing a 17lb shot were in hand and by May 1942 the 17-pounder gun was introduced. Hurriedly fitted to 25-pounder field gun carriages, as the split trail carriage was not ready, about a hundred were rushed to the Mediterranean to counter the appearance of the German Tiger tank the following year. By mid-1944 the 17-pounder had become the mainstay of the anti-tank regiments of the British and Canadian armies.

It had been hoped as early as 1942 to use the Bishop (a 25-pounder self-propelled gun based on the Valentine chassis) as a mounting for the new 17-pounder, but this was not possible and instead the British Army ended up with the rear-facing Archer variant. While it was far from perfect, 665 examples of the latter were constructed from 1944 to 1945. An experimental self-propelled wheeled mounting was designed by Nicholas Straussler for the gun in 1943. This used a motive unit based on Bedford QL lorry components, but it was not taken up because it was felt it left the crew too exposed when in combat.

The Challenger cruiser tank was also armed with the 17-pounder and 200 of these were ordered and saw action in northwest Europe. Probably the most famous 17-pounder anti-tank gun mounting was the Sherman Firefly VC, which was developed to make up for the slow pace of the Challenger. By June 1944 it was the only Allied tank capable of taking on the German Panther and Tiger. Similarly, the British Comet was armed with a shortened version of the 17-pounder, but the 77mm gun did not have the penetrating power of the latter.

The Soviets were well prepared, as Red Army veteran Mansur Abdulin recorded in his memoirs: 'We knew all the technical characteristics of Tigers, Panthers, Ferdinands and other enemy tanks and self-propelled guns. Our gunners received new anti-tank weapons. We also became acquainted with new self-propelled 152mm guns. ... We veterans explained to the greenhorns the particular weaknesses ...'.

The T-34/85 was deployed in conjunction with an 85mm self-propelled gun mounted on the T-34 chassis and known as the SU-85. This heavily armoured assault gun appeared in the battles in Ukraine in 1944 and was subsequently replaced by the SU-100 mounting a more powerful 100mm M1944 field gun.

The Russians introduced only one new tank, the IS (also known as JS) or Iosef Stalin, although in truth this was not an entirely new design, rather a redesigned KV. Although classed as a heavy tank, it was actually roughly the same weight as the Panther medium tank. The IS-1 or IS-85 (after the calibre of its gun) was developed

The British Ordnance QF 17-pounder anti-tank gun posed the greatest threat to the Tiger.

Another view of the same weapon showing the split trail. The guns sent to North Africa to counter the Tunisian Tigers were on 25-pounder carriages.

alongside the KV-85 and entered service in September 1943. The IS was initially equipped with an 85mm gun, then a 100mm gun, and finally a 122mm gun, enabling Soviet tank crews to engage any German tank type at extremely long ranges. The IS-2 went into production in late 1943; only 102 were produced in that year, but in 1944 Soviet factories churned out 2,250. The up-gunned IS-2 first saw action in the Ukraine in early 1944, 'claiming' forty-one Tigers and Elefants for the loss of only eight tanks. While the panzers could knock out the IS-2, they had no real answer to its 122mm armament, which easily outgunned them.

It has been calculated that in total eighteen units equipped with Tiger Is and Tiger IIs accounted for 9,850 kills, for the loss of 1,715 tanks. The kill-to-loss ratio, although varying quite widely from unit to unit, averaged almost 6:1. This clearly made a nonsense of the Allies' preferred 3:1 ratio when taking on a Tiger. Despite Allied tankers' fear of the Tiger, they soon learned that it was vulnerable on the flanks and at close range. The only way to neutralise a Tiger was to stalk it and attack from close range.

The Soviets greatly respected the Tiger, but were quick to develop ways of overcoming its capabilities, often at great personal cost. Soviet tankers had to close down the 1,000m range of the 88mm gun as quickly as possible, and this meant a nerve-wracking charge towards the frontal armour of a Tiger in a desperate bid to close with it before being hit. If there were enough T-34s, then the Tiger was at risk of being swamped no matter how many enemy tanks it knocked out, especially if it did not withdraw quickly enough.

At Kursk General Rotmistrov recalled, 'Our tanks were destroying the Tigers at close range ... We knew their vulnerable spots, so our tank crews were firing at their sides. The shells fired from very short distances tore large holes in the armour of the Tigers.'

In describing the battle of Kursk, the Soviet Official History graphically recorded:

The battlefield seemed too small for the hundreds of armoured machines. Groups of tanks moved over the steppe, taking cover behind isolated groves and orchards. The detonations of the guns merged into a continuous menacing growl.

The tanks of the 5th Guards Tank Army cut into the Nazi development at full speed. This attack was so fast that the enemy did not have time to prepare to meet it, and the leading ranks of the Soviet tanks passed right through the enemy's entire first echelon, destroying his leading units and sub-units. The Tigers, deprived in close combat of the advantages which their powerful gun and thick armour conferred, were successfully shot-up by T-34s at close range. Immense numbers of tanks were mixed up all over the battlefield, and there was neither time nor space to disengage and reform the ranks. Shells fired at short range penetrated both the front and side armour of the tanks. While this

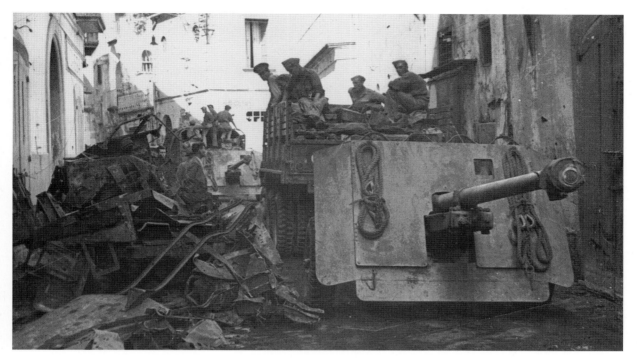

These 17-pounder guns were photographed in Italy during the push on Naples.

was going on, there were frequent explosions as ammunition blew up, while tank turrets, blown off by the force of the explosions, were thrown dozens of yards away from the twisted machines.

Recounting the bitter fighting between the Soviet 181st Tank Brigade and the 1st SS Panzer Division, the Official History observes that the Soviet tankers showed incredible bravery and sacrifice:

The 2nd Battalion of the 181st Brigade, 18th Tanks Corps, attacking along the left bank of the Psel, clashed with a group of Tigers [led by Michael Wittmann], which met the Soviet tanks with fire from the halt ... Several Tigers opened fire on Skripkin's tank simultaneously. One enemy shell punctured the side, another wounded the commander. The driver-mechanic and radio operator dragged him out of the tank and hid him in a shell hole. But one of the Tigers was heading straight for them. The driver-mechanic, Alexander Nikolayev, jumped back into his damaged and burning tank, started the engine and rushed headlong at the enemy. It was as if a ball of fire careered over the battlefield. The Tigers stopped, hesitated, began to turn away. But it was too late. At full speed the burning KV [tank] smashed into the German tank. The explosion shook the earth. This ramming so shook the Nazis that they began a hasty withdrawal.

The British also mounted the 17-pounder in the Sherman to create the Firefly, but in a stand-up fight with a Tiger its armour was wholly inadequate.

At Prokhorovka Soviet troops even resorted to using two grenades and a Molotov cocktail in a bundle dubbed 'a bottle of Champagne for a hangover!' to take out Tigers. Veteran Mansur Abdulin remembers how one comrade, Kostia Martynov, desperate to claim a Tiger, dug a trench some 30 metres away out in no-man's-land.

> We see Kostia jump out of his trench and throw the bundle of explosives underneath the caterpillar of the tank. It seems to us that Kostia has plenty of time to take cover before the blast. Then comes the powerful defeating explosion. The Tiger loses its track and twitches, trying to resume its forward movement. But having only one caterpillar, it turns and collapses on its side. Our boys bring some fresh 'Champagne' bottles and soon the Tiger is in flames.

The engagement cost the Germans two Tigers and Kostia his life.

While Allied tank crews were learning how to stalk the Tiger, it often pounced first. Colonel Henry E. Gardiner, commander of the 2nd Battalion, 13th Armored Regiment, US 1st Armored Division, had the unpleasant experience of being surprised by a Tiger in Tunisia. Fighting in an M3 Grant, he had just knocked out a panzer when he recalled,

Just at that point we were hit hard by what later proved to be 88mm fire from a Tiger tank that I had not seen. The M3 had a crew of seven. The driver and gunner were killed, the assistant driver badly wounded and I got some shrapnel in my left arm. The other three men escaped without injury. .... I was evacuated to a British tent field hospital near Bone where most of the shrapnel was removed from my arm and after a week I rejoined my battalion.

In the close-quarter tank battles fought among Normandy's hedgerows in the summer of 1944 British tank crews were under no illusions about their vulnerability to the Tiger's 88mm gun. Even if the crew survived a hit, they were likely to be machine-gunned as they baled out and into the nearest ditch. The Tiger I sealed its reputation in Normandy at the engagement at Villers-Bocage, though Allied tank crews were already afraid of it.

Colin Thomson, an armoured car driver-operator with the 11th Hussars, recalled,

My troop penetrated ... as far as Cahagnes where ... we saw a large concentration of enemy armour moving towards Villers-Bocage. Round the corner of a narrow lane came a German 8-wheel armoured car ... Our lead car gunner let go. The Jerry vehicle went up in a cloud of smoke.

A rear view of a Sherman Firefly, somewhere in Germany.

This British Achilles, also armed with the 17-pounder gun, was photographed in October 1944 engaging enemy pillboxes along the German frontier. Its unit had claimed twenty-one panzers.

We heard another vehicle ... 'Please God, it's not a Tiger!' someone said. It turned out to be a huge self-propelled gun which we hit with everything we had, destroying it and its crew.

The 8th Hussars to the north advanced to help, but were engaged by four Tigers; they suffered heavy losses and were driven off. Colin Thomson observed, 'By the time we reached the outskirts reports spoke of extremely hard fighting there. We began to work up north and north-west and also to the south where, at Tracy-Bocage, the troops came under fire from 88mms.'

Michael Wittmann, while attacking Villers-Bocage a second time with two Tigers and a Panzer IV, drove straight into a British ambush. 'When the Tigers were about 1,000 yards away and were broadside to us I told 3 Troop and my gunner to fire,' recalled Lieutenant Bill Cotton. 'The Firefly [with a 17-pounder gun] did the damage, but the 75s helped and must have taken a track off one, which started to circle out of control.'

A towed anti-tank gun hit Wittmann's tank, and the following Tiger was caught by Sergeant Bobby Bramall's Firefly; Corporal Horne's Cromwell missed the target, and the Panzer IV had almost got past the second Tiger when Horne drove out behind the German and blasted him. A third Tiger entered the town but was also caught by B Squadron a few dozen yards from the main street at the crossroads of the rue Jeanne Bacon and rue Emile Samson.

The Tigers were quick to react. 'They shot back at us, and knocked the Firefly out, as its commander was hit in the head,' said Lieutenant Cotton. 'However, at the end of a very few minutes there were three "killed" Tigers.' The crews escaped because too few British infantry remained to take them prisoner. Later Cotton, armed with an umbrella, and with Bramall carrying blankets and petrol, walked in the pouring rain to the panzers and set fire to them to prevent recovery – something the Germans were very adept at.

At about 1700 hours on the 13th, while the Tigers were regrouping, the British withdrew to Tracy-Bocage, 2 miles to the west, having lost twenty-five tanks and twenty-eight armoured fighting vehicles. B Squadron was ordered to time its withdrawal to coincide with a covering barrage that would be laid down on the town. Stan Lockwood had just driven his Firefly across the town square when it stalled. Fortunately Sergeant Bill Moore in the following tank jumped down under small arms fire and attached a tow cable to Lockwood's tank, towing him out just before the bombardment began.

Second Lieutenant Stuart Hill recalled his regiment, the Nottinghamshire Sherwood Rangers Yeomanry, equipped with Sherman tanks, tangling with the Tiger in Normandy on 26 June 1944:

As they cleared Fontenay, they were suddenly confronted by an enormous tank coming round the bend in front. It was hard to know who was more surprised,

This unsatisfactory interim Tiger killer is the Archer, which married the 17-pounder gun with the Valentine tank chassis and joined the British Army in October 1944. The gun faced to the rear of the vehicle.

The American M5 3in (76.2mm) anti-tank gun was the only towed weapon bigger than the standard 57mm anti-tank gun. It was also installed in the M10 tank-destroyer.

The M10 Gun Motor Carriage was armed with the 3in M7 gun that could tackle a Tiger, but it lacked adequate armour, like the Firefly.

but John [Semken, commanding A Squadron] shrieked, 'Fire, it's a Hun', and they loosed off about ten rounds into the smoke. As this cleared away, it was observed that the crew were baling out as small flames came from inside the tank. It was a Tiger of 12th SS Panzer, the first Tiger to be captured in Normandy, and it made an impressive sight at close quarters as both its size and the thickness of its armour became apparent. Although the range had been only 60 yards, not one Sherman shell had penetrated that armour. The fire in the Tiger, we discovered, had instead been caused by a shot hitting the side of the driver's observation visor and showering white-hot splinters into the tank. The driver screamed that he had been hit and the commander obligingly ordered his crew out.

A Squadron claimed a Tiger, a Panther and thirteen Panzer IVs. The following day B Squadron pushed on to Rauray. Resuming his account, Stuart Hill recalled, 'By midday Rauray had been cleared and in it were found about eight German tanks, all damaged to some extent, and one of them a Tiger, which seemed to be in perfect working order. We tried to incorporate it into our ranks, but unfortunately the High Command wanted it to be taken back to England.'

Some Shermans were fitted with a 76mm gun from February 1944 in time for the northwest Europe campaign.

A real Tiger killer in the shape of the M26 Pershing armed with a 90mm gun appeared in the closing months of the Second World War.

Hill had a close shave involving a Tiger on 2 August:

The column halted to allow the sappers to come up and clear the mines, when suddenly a Tiger tank emerged from cover and moved to the high ground overlooking the road. It opened fire at about 2,000 yards and hit a tank further back in the column. With both ends of the road now blocked, we were bottled up and the Tiger was out of our range.

I shouted: 'Gunner, traverse right. Steady on Tiger. Smoke. 1,750 yards. Fire when ready.' Our shot landed just in front of the Tiger and the smoke soon obscured it from view. We fired again, this time just to the left of the tank, aiming to keep plenty of smoke between us and it. Other tank commanders did the same, while the air officer accompanying us called up four Typhoon fighter-bombers off the cab-rank to fire their rockets at the Tiger. We fired some red smoke to identify the target, and then the planes came in, very low and with a tremendous roar. The second plane scored a direct hit and, when the smoke cleared, we could see the Tiger lying on its side minus its turret and with no sign of any survivors.

Ultimately it took guts and nerves of steel to kill a Tiger at close quarters, as Hill observed: 'Sergeant George Dring, that inveterate destroyer of tanks, stalked a Tiger on foot and then directed his own tank to kill it. Two other Tigers, heavily bogged down in wet ground, were captured intact.'

The Tiger finally met its match on 26 February 1945 when the American M26 Pershing tank went into action with the US 3rd Armored Division. The first encounter did not go well for the Americans, who were guarding a roadblock. A Tiger lurking behind a building just 100 yards away got off three shots. The first 88mm round burst into the Pershing's turret through the co-axial machine gun port, killing the gunner and the loader. The following shot caught the muzzle break of the 90mm gun, setting off the round in the chamber. The third shot glanced off the right side of the turret and tore off the upper cupola hatch, which had been left open. Ironically, the Tiger then tried to beat a hasty retreat, only to become entangled in a pile of debris and the crew fled.

Shortly afterwards Sergeant Nick Mashlonik recalled stalking a Tiger:

Our first exposure to the enemy with the new M26 was very fruitful. We were hit hard by the Germans from Elsdorf. The enemy appeared to have much armour as we received a lot of direct fire and this kept us pinned down. Our casualties kept mounting and the Commanding Officer of our company asked me if I thought I could knock the Tiger out that was almost destroying us. The Company Commander and I did some investigating, by crawling out to a position where we could see from ground level a sight to behold. The German

Soviet attempts to counter the Tiger included the SU-85/100 tank-destroyer, which married an 85mm/100mm gun to the T-34 chassis respectively.

The ISU-122/152 gained the nickname 'Beast-killer' for its effectiveness against the Tiger and the Panther.

The IS-2 with its huge 122mm gun was easily able to overcome the Tiger and was produced in far greater numbers.

Tiger was slightly dug in and this meant it would be more difficult to destroy. I decided that I could take this Tiger with my 90mm.

Our M26 was in defilade position, more or less hidden in a little valley. I detailed my driver Cade and gunner Gormick to accompany me on this mission. I would be gunner and have Gormick load. I instructed both of them that once we had fired three shots – two armour piercing and one HE [High Explosive] point detonating – we would immediately back up so as not to expose ourselves too long on the top of the hill.

Just as we started our tank and moved very slowly forward (creeping), I noticed that the German Tiger was moving out of the position and exposed his belly to us. I immediately put a shell into its belly and knocked it off. The second shot was fired at his track and knocked his right track off. The third shot was fired at his turret with HE point detonating and destroyed the escaping crew.

The Tiger was the first of the heavy tanks; although it stole a march on the Allies, it was never produced in sufficient numbers. Nazi Germany was already facing defeat by the time the American Pershing and Soviet Joseph Stalin heavy tanks appeared. British attempts at producing a tank with sufficient firepower in the shape of the Archer, Challenger, Comet and Firefly were little more than inadequate stopgaps.

Epilogue

Tiger's Big Brother: Maus

The US 80th Infantry Division overran the city of Kassel in early April 1945 and along with it the Henschel and Wegmann works, finally ending Tiger II production. The Kassel factories still had 15,000 workers on its books, including 8,000 who had been involved in Tiger and Panther production. American soldiers were able to wander around the assembly lines where uncompleted panzers lay abandoned. The spindle borers, radial drills and turret drills were impressive pieces of machinery and offered testimony to the fine precision that had produced the Tigers.

With the advent of the Tiger I, Hitler allowed his designers to abandon the balance between firepower, armour and mobility by placing greater emphasis on firepower and armour. Certainly the armour and the gun were first class. While the Tiger's speed was not a real problem, its weight certainly was, as it put a strain on the drivetrain, gearbox and engine. Its weight meant that if it bogged down or flipped over it was very difficult to recover. Bridges struggled to withstand the burden and, while the Tiger could physically demolish a house unscratched, it could easily drop through the floor. In addition, Tiger tanks were regularly captured because they were too heavy to rescue from the battlefield.

In North Africa the British Army had marvelled at Rommel's tank-recovery capabilities and his supporting field maintenance depots. Time and time again he was able to rescue damaged and stranded tanks and get them back into action. This could make all the difference between winning and losing a tank battle. During the initial stages of the Normandy campaign and in the fighting on the Eastern Front German recovery rates were still good.

The Tiger had practically no dedicated recovery infrastructure or specialised vehicles to help. The German armed forces lacked heavy tank transporters, which meant the Tiger had to get to the front under its own power and often broke down before it even got there. Due to the lack of purpose-built recovery vehicles, three heavy-duty half-tracks were needed to budge an immobilised Tiger. Using another Tiger inevitably led to its engine overheating. If the tank's tracks overrode the sprockets and jammed, it took two Tigers to drag the disabled one. Getting the broken track off was also a major headache for the crews and their mechanics. None of these time-consuming activities was really possible while under fire. All the crew could do if their Tiger was disabled and they survived was abandon ship.

The Tiger II suffered the same problems, especially where the drivetrain was concerned. Nonetheless strenuous efforts were made to address many of the Tiger II's problems. Notably its availability became almost as good as that of the Panzer IV, and for its size its agility was also quite good. In contrast, the Jagdtiger proved to be pretty much an unmitigated disaster. At almost 72 tons, it was the heaviest armoured fighting vehicle of the Second World War. It was too immobile and was simply abandoned by its poorly trained crews at the roadside. To be fair, although dubbed a hunting tank, it was not a tank at all but a tank-destroyer in the same mould as the German Army's dedicated anti-tank assault guns and self-propelled guns. The French tank museum at Saumur has the only running Tiger II and the Tank Museum at Bovington has one of the few remaining Jagdtigers.

The 60-ton Tiger I and 70-ton Tiger II were not to have been the end of the Tiger story. Up until the summer of 1944 Hitler had plans for a successor tank that would have been at least twice the weight and with a gun twice as big. While the Tiger series set the trend for tanks sporting ever larger anti-tank weapons and thicker armour, their legacy was actually quite short-lived. Ultimately, there is a limit in the weight to armament ratio that can be achieved with tanks. Certainly the Tiger I and II were great successes compared to Hitler's more harebrained schemes. No other armies ever followed up on his flirtation with super-heavy tanks such as the proposed Panzer VII Löwe (Lion) and Panzer VIII Maus (Mouse).

The Löwe never progressed any further than a single prototype chassis, and in the case of the enormous Maus its ridiculous weight of almost 200 tons ensured it never went into production. Hitler had wanted 150 of the things. Likewise the 140-ton E-100 never came to fruition. The latter drawing on the Tiger series would have essentially looked like a scaled-up Tiger II. The plan was that the Maus would be armed with a 128mm gun and the E-100 with a 150mm gun. Similarly, plans for a Tiger II self-propelled gun got no further than a prototype chassis at the very end of the war.

Where the Maus was concerned, Hitler had completely lost the plot, as it would have fallen through almost every bridge it tried to cross. Making it submersible is unlikely to have solved the problem: Europe's mighty rivers would have made short work of the Maus. Had it seen the light of day, its fate on the battlefield would have been similar to that of the Soviet KV-1 and KV-2. Wasting design and production effort on the Maus and E-100, two separate and competing heavy tanks, at such a crucial stage of the war was inexcusable – but that was Hitler's way of doing things, as witnessed during his development of the Tiger I with both Henschel and Porsche vying for the contract. It is likely that these super-heavy tanks would have been just as burdensome to build as the Tiger I and II. But at a time when he was losing the tank production war, even Hitler came to his senses.

These projects are quite remarkable when you consider that German tank development and theories for their use were so radical in 1940–41. Yet between 1942 and 1945, despite the wealth of battlefield experience, it seemed as if panzer development was going backwards, having increasingly sacrificed mobility for firepower. If Hitler had had his way, the Tiger series would have been just the tip of the proverbial iceberg. To what end is difficult to fathom, but of course by 1944 Hitler was increasingly desperate to fend off the encroaching Red Army and its proven T-34.

Hitler was largely on his own in his conviction that heavy tanks were a good thing. The Soviets initially abandoned heavy tanks after their unsuccessful T-35 and KV proved to be lumbering liabilities in the face of the Nazi Blitzkrieg. The British TOG, A33 and Tortoise and American M6 and T-28 also proved to be developmental dead ends. They were all deemed to be of extremely limited tactical value.

Hitler finally called a halt to the development of his super-heavy tanks in 1944, though his designers continued to tinker until the very end of the war. The two Maus prototypes were unceremoniously blown up at Kummersdorf. The only heavy tanks to appear in the closing days of the Second World War were the American M26 Pershing and Soviet Joseph Stalin, and both proved equal to the Tiger. However, their post-war service was very limited.

Even if the design limitations could have been overcome, the concept of a Durchbruchwagen or heavy breakthrough tank was a luxury that armies could ill-afford. Only the Soviet IS-2, which went into action in 1944 armed with a 122mm gun and was lighter than the Tiger, was employed in a breakthrough role. Most modern armies settled for a main battle tank in the 60-tons range with a gun of around 125mm calibre.

Modern tanks are very costly to build and few nations have the desire or need to deploy more than one tank type. What is needed is a good all-rounder. Nonetheless the public myth that the Tiger was some sort of super-tank remains undiminished. Such is the enduring fascination with it that in 2011 a Russian film production company built an exact replica of a Tiger I from scratch – clearly cost was no object. In the UK the imposing presence of the restored Tiger 131 and the Tiger II at the British Tank Museum as always remain major crowd-pleasers.

Further Reading

Ford, Roger, *Weapons at War – the Tiger Tank* (History Press Ltd, 1998)

Forty, George, *Tiger Tank Battalions in World War II* (Motor Books International, 2008)

Gander, Terry J., *Tanks in detail: Pzkpfw VI Ausf E & B Panzer VI Tiger I & II* (Ian Allen, 2003)

Gander, Terry J., *Tanks in detail: JgdPz IV, V, VI and Hetzer Jagdpanzer* (Ian Allen, 2004)

Green, Michael and Brown, James, *Tiger Tanks at War* (Motorbooks International, 2008)

Hayton, Michael, *Tiger Tank Manual, Panzerkampfwagen VI Tiger I Ausf E (Sdkfz 181)*, Owners Workshop Manual (Haynes, 2011)

Jentz, Thomas L. and Doyle, Hilary L., *Germany's Tiger Tanks* (Schiffer Publishing, 2004)

Jentz, Thomas L., Doyle, Hilary L. and Sarson, Peter, *Tiger I Heavy Tanks 1942–1945* (Osprey, 1993)

Kleine, Egon and Kuhn, Volkmar, *Tiger: the History of a Legendary Weapon 1942–45* (J.J. Fedorwicz Publishing, 1989)

Spielberger, Walter J., *Tiger & King Tiger Tanks and their Variants* (Haynes, 1991)

Useful Websites:

Achtung Panzer!: www.achtungpanzer.com

Tiger Battalions: www.fprado.com/armorsite/tigers.htm

Tiger I Information Center: www.alanhamby.com/tiger.html